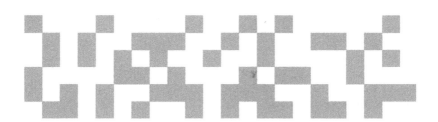

Values and Vulnerabilities

The Ethics of Research with Refugees and Asylum Seekers

Karen Block, Elisha Riggs & Nick Haslam, Editors

AUSTRALIANACADEMIC S

First published in 2013 by Australian Academic Press
Level 5, Toowong Tower, — 9 Sherwood Road,
Toowong QLD 4066, Australia
www.australianacademicpress.com.au

National Library of Australia Cataloguing-in-Publication entry:

Title: Values and vulnerabilities : the ethics of research with
                refugees and asylum seekers / Karen Block, Elisha Riggs, and
                Nick Haslam, editors.

Edition: First Edition

ISBN: 9781922117137 (Paperback)
                9781922117144 (eBook)

Subjects: Political refugees--Research.
                Refugees--Research.

Other Authors   Block, Karen, editor.
/Contributors: Riggs, Elisha, editor.
                Haslam, Nick, 1963- editor.

Dewey Number: 342.083

Book and cover design by Maria Biaggini — The Letter Tree.

CONTENTS

PART 3

ADVOCACY AND POLITICS
— CONSIDERING THE RAMIFICATIONS OF RESEARCH

FOREWORD

We live in a time when the numbers of people forced to flee for their lives by violence and adversity is greater than ever — yet the proportion granted asylum as refugees has declined. While there have been heated debates in wealthy countries about how to honour humanitarian goals and international commitments for asylum, most of those forced to migrate are internally displaced people struggling to survive in regions of impoverished, war-torn countries that can afford them little protection. Many who would avail themselves of refugee status are unable to find any safe haven and continue to be exposed to violence, privation and profound uncertainty about their fate.

The category of refugees is not intrinsic to any individual's personhood or identity. Refugees are forcibly made by the actions of others: first by the violence that propels them from their homes, then by the international conventions that define the category of refugee and finally, by the immigration policies of countries that provide asylum. The 1951 UN Convention Relating to the Status of Refugees recognised the right of individuals facing persecution by reason of race, religion, nationality, membership of a particular social group or political opinion to seek asylum and the obligation of nations to provide this safe haven. Refugee rights represent an important step in building a global community founded on respect for human life and on basic notions of equity, equality, and responsibility.

Serious engagement with the predicament of refugees comes from an ethical position of universalism, based on the thought experiment of substitution — what if it was me or my family in that situation? In making this shift in perspective, we are limited by our imagination and by our willingness to recognise that our positions of privilege are not earned but accidental. Our safety, power and privilege are accidents of history and geography, outcomes of an implicit 'birthright lottery' that has resulted in our relative advantage. For those of us who live in wealthy and peaceful countries, it is tempting to view our good fortune as due to our own virtue or the wise choices and hard work of our ancestors. In this way, our privilege is justified and the sense of a just moral order is maintained. Unfortunately, the evidence is everywhere at hand that resources have not been evenly distributed on the basis of need, merit or any notion of justice. The world is a manifestly unfair place with inhumane inequities reflecting the historical violence of colonisation, racism, war and exploitation. Indeed, it is not hard to show that much of our relative advantage stems directly from enduring forms of structural violence rooted in this violent history. Globalisation, as much as it increases the mobility of information and opportunity, acts in many ways to exacerbate these inequalities.

Recognising this history should motivate us all to shelter those most acutely in need. Yet, the current climate of fear and suspicion has challenged and in some places actively undermined our modest steps toward respecting human rights and equity. The current plight of refugees reflects a global regime of insecurity that increasingly views strangers as potential vectors of terror and disruption, threats to a secular social order, or, at best, as a burdensome drain on resources.

The contributors to this volume have thought long and hard about the dilemmas posed by the refugee's predicament and seek ways to use research to understand the impact of human rights, law and governmental practices, to chart the trajectories of survival and resilience and discover ways to mitigate the impact of policies of deterrence, exclusion and harsh treatment that abound. As the editors note, three central themes run throughout the book: *vulnerability*, both as risk for illness but also as a call to ethical action and responsibility; *power*, both political and professional; and the relationship between *research and advocacy* which calls for active efforts by professionals and others to make common cause and support agency of people who have lost their homes.

There is an ethics of vulnerability, that recognises the imperative to protect and also the danger of treating the other as 'needy', the passive recipient of our care and concern. Viewing whole groups or categories of people as vulnerable may be disparaging and further undermine their autonomy and agency. Yet there are forms of vulnerability that are intrinsic to the human condition. Here is helpful to invoke the work of the philosopher Emmanuel Levinas, who insisted that ethical being begins with our recognition of the vulnerability of the other. Levinas was fundamentality concerned with the problem of alterity or otherness — of the sense that, as much as we share a common humanity with others, each of us is also a stranger. Indeed, at times of extremity or when probing more deeply, we are all strangers to ourselves. A Levinasian ethic would view vulnerability not as risk but as recognition of the naked face which presents the other as vulnerable to be misheard, misread, or mistaken for another. Of course, for refugees this vulnerability has its own extremities that come from being stateless, deterritorialised without claim to space or place unless it is through the hospitality of others. The response to the refugee as a vulnerable stranger is then a measure of our basic capacity for ethical awareness and commitment.

The paradox of vulnerability is that even as it defines the category of refugee and legitimates their claims for asylum, it consigns them to the disempowered position of passive recipient of gifts bestowed by the wealthy and powerful other. Asylum seekers are seen as hapless victims of circumstances beyond their control, driven by necessity, with few options and less choice. To the extent that refugees are viewed as having agency

— making choices, planning their escape, seeking to secure asylum, and especially looking forward and trying to insure a secure life for themselves and their families—they may be suspect. Their very planfulness undermines the perceived legitimacy of their claim. This sets up a vicious circle that undermines strength and resilience vulnerability — since, precisely to the extent refugees are agentic, strategic, and future-oriented they are perceived as manipulative and less worthy of protection and support. Evidence of agency undermines legitimacy in a morally driven cycle of delegitimation that seems perversely calculated to undermine adaptation and long-term outcome for refugees.

There is a crucial issue of voice, of who speaks for the refugee or asylum seeker – not only because they are in a precarious position that affords them little opportunity to be heard but also because the stories they have to tell may be difficult for those firmly ensconced in situations of comfort and privilege to begin to understand. There is a quotidian violence that comes from non-recognition, turning away from witnessing the refugee's predicament, disparaging or trivialising it or co-opting it for local political gain. To counter this non-recognition, there is a need to represent, mediate and give space to voices of those who are marginalised, neglected or actively silenced by others who do not want to hear their stories.

As the contributions to this volume show, the research process can give voice and agency to refugees. Participatory action research aims to support the refugee's agency. Work that documents the impact of detention or deterrence on long-term mental health can guide policy that is humane and yields the best outcomes. However, refugee research faces problems of credibility on several fronts including questions related to ethics, methodology, and epistemology. Most research is done by people identified with advocacy, hence there may be presumptions of bias. Refugee research can be extraordinarily difficult because of issues of access and constraints due to the nature of the settings, which include both detention camps and impenetrable bureaucracies pre-occupied with justifying or defending the status quo. Moreover, the refugee situation is inherently dynamic spanning a long and perilous trajectory of seeking asylum, the prolonged uncertainty of refugee determination, the continuing vulnerability of family and friends still in harm's way, and the challenges of rebuilding a life after forced migration. Crucial outcomes may only be known after months, years or decades, demanding sustained commitments to research over time spans that may exceed the cycles of granting agencies or electoral politics.

Although the issues addressed in this volume should be the concern of all citizens, it is clear that researchers, health professionals, and others who produce knowledge and wield specific forms of clinical power and scientific authority have an important role to play in addressing the dilemmas of refugee health, security and well-being. Thinking through the ethical issues of refugee research clears the way to producing knowledge that can guide humane policy that respects the need for asylum. In so doing, we have the opportunity to advance the vision of human community and solidarity inherent in human rights. Ultimately, our capacity to provide refuge says much about the moral quality or climate of our communities — as our humanity is tested by our response to the strangers at the gate.

Laurence J. Kirmayer

NOTES ON CONTRIBUTORS

Mammad Aidani has taught and conducted research in the University of Melbourne in the School of Historical and Philosophical Studies. He taught in the Department of Performance and Theatre Studies at Victoria University and worked as the Director of the Writing Department at the Footscray Community Arts Centre. He has a PhD in Hermeneutics and Phenomenological Philosophy and Narrative Psychology. His recent publications include the book *Welcoming the Stranger: Narratives of Identity and Belonging in an Iranian Diaspora* (Common Ground, 2010) and a number of journal articles on related topics. As part of his ARC Research Fellowship, his current research focuses on perceptions, interpretations and ways of trauma and suffering among Iranian diaspora men.

Linda Bartolomei is the Deputy Director of the Centre for Refugee Research (CRR) and the Coordinator of the Master in Social Development at the University of New South Wales. Since 2002, Linda has been engaged in a series of action research based projects with refugee and displaced communities across the world. A major focus of her work has been with women and girls who have survived rape and sexual violence in refugee and conflict situations.

Karen Block is a research fellow in the Jack Brockhoff Child Health and Wellbeing Program, McCaughey VicHealth Centre, Melbourne School of Population Health, University of Melbourne. Karen has a background spanning clinical sciences, history, languages and the sociology of health with an interest in research methodologies and ethics. Her research is focused on understanding the social determinants of health and wellbeing for refugee-background young people in the settlement context. Recent publication topics include work on ethical strategies for engaging refugee youth in research (*Journal of Refugee Studies*) and the social and learning environment in schools (*Health Education & Behavior*).

Sandy Gifford is Professor of Anthropology and Refugee Studies at the Swinburne Institute for Social Research. She is an anthropologist with a research focus on settlement, wellbeing, policy and practice among humanitarian migrants in Australia with a particular focus on young people. She has published on ethnographic mixed method longitudinal studies of refugee settlement (*Journal of Refugee Studies*), refugee wellbeing and belonging (*Social Science and Medicine*) and refugee youth identity (*Journal of Youth Studies*). Her current research includes a study of digital media in connecting refugee youth with their families still overseas and an ethnography of Australia's refugee settlement program.

Lynn Gillam is an ethicist with particular interests in clinical ethics, research ethics and ethics education. Lynn is the Academic Director of the Children's Bioethics Centre, an initiative of the Royal Children's Hospital Melbourne, in partnership with the Murdoch Children's Research Institute and the University of Melbourne. As part of this role, she is the clinical ethicist at the Royal Children's Hospital. At the University of Melbourne, Lynn is Associate Professor in Health Ethics at the Centre for Health and Society, in the Melbourne School of Population Health, where she teaches health ethics in the medical curriculum and the postgraduate social health program. She is the chair of the University of Melbourne Human Research Ethics Committee, and has published widely on research ethics.

Hariz Halilovich, PhD, is a sociocultural anthropologist and an award-winning writer, currently working as a senior lecturer at Monash University, Melbourne, Australia. Prior to Monash University, he worked in teaching and research positions at the University of Melbourne and RMIT University. His research and teaching interests have been primarily in the areas of migration (including forced, internal and cross-border migration), memory, human rights and reconciliation. This research informs his approaches to teaching, which see students engage in experiential learning, field-based studies and intercultural learning in order to better understand self and community. His forthcoming book *Places of Pain* is published by Berghahn Books.

Nick Haslam is Professor of Psychology at the University of Melbourne. He received his PhD in social and clinical psychology from the University of Pennsylvania and then taught for several years at the New School for Social Research. His research has addressed social perception, dehumanisation, prejudice, and psychiatric classification. His six previous books include the title *Introduction to Personality and Intelligence* and *Yearning to Breathe Free: Seeking Asylum in Australia* (with Dean Lusher). His meta-analytic research on refugee mental health with Matt Porter has been published in *JAMA: The Journal of the American Medical Association.*

Ida Kaplan is Direct Services Manager, Victorian Foundation for Survivors of Torture (VFST). In that role she oversees client services, is involved in the development of service models for refugees and asylum seekers and has had extensive experience, locally and internationally training professionals in the provision of appropriate interventions for survivors of torture and trauma. She has a longstanding policy, practice and research interest in the intersection of mental health, social justice and human rights issues in understanding recovery from trauma. She and her colleagues have published research on the effects of long-term detention.

Laurence J. Kirmayer is James McGill Professor and Director, Division of Social and Transcultural Psychiatry, Department of Psychiatry, McGill University. He is editor-in-chief of *Transcultural Psychiatry*, and Director of the Culture and Mental Health Research Unit, Jewish General Hospital in Montreal, where he conducts research on mental health services for immigrants and refugees, psychiatry in primary care, the mental health of indigenous peoples, and the anthropology of psychiatry. His past research includes studies on pathways and barriers to mental health care for immigrants and refugees, and cultural concepts of mental health and illness. He co-edited *Current Concepts of Somatization, Understanding Trauma: Integrating Biological, Clinical, and Cultural Perspectives*, and *Healing Traditions: The Mental Health of Aboriginal Peoples in Canada*.

Jeanette Lawrence is an associate professor in the Melbourne School of Psychological Sciences. She is a developmental psychologist. Her primary research interests are in persons and their interactions with their social environments. This includes published work and ongoing studies in the areas of the developmental experiences of young people from refugee backgrounds, especially in relation to culture and social institutions; intergenerational relations across the life-span; and children and the law, particularly in relation to child protection.

Marinella Marmo is an associate professor in Criminal Justice at Flinders University Law School. She previously lectured at the University of Leicester and the Liverpool John Moores University (UK). She has been a visiting scholar at The Chinese Academy of Social Science (China), Roma Tre University (Italy), Umea University (Sweden). She has published in several journals such as *Gender & History, Law Text Culture* and *International Journal of Comparative and Applied*

Criminal Justice. In 2011, she co-edited *Crime and Justice: A Guide to Criminology.* Her research has been widely cited in numerous newspapers, including *The Guardian* and *The New York Times.*

Christopher McDowell is a Reader in Political Anthropology at City University London. He has published widely on forced population displacement, asylum and involuntary resettlement in Africa, Asia and Europe. Recent publications include *Displacement: The Human Cost of Development and Resettlement* (2012 Palgrave) with Olivia Bennett, and *Non-Conflict Displacement: Challenges for the 21st Century* (2010 Berghahn) with Gareth Morrell. Christopher is currently researching forced collectivisation in Soviet Kirghizia, Central Asia.

Colleen McFarlane is a clinical psychologist and research fellow with the Victorian Foundation for Survivors of Torture. She has been involved in the delivery and evaluation of psychosocial services for clients with refugee and asylum seeker backgrounds for 10 years. Her research and clinical interests lie in the areas of interventions for torture and trauma, cross-cultural psychology, and qualitative methods. She and her colleagues have published work about indicators of wellbeing for children with a refugee background.

Louise Newman is Professor of Developmental Psychiatry at Monash University, and Director of the Centre for Developmental Psychiatry and Psychology. She is current Chair of the Detention Expert Health Advisory Group, an independent body providing advice to the Australian Department of Immigration and Citizenship on the health and mental health needs of asylum seekers. Her research looks at the psychological impact of trauma and the mental health needs of asylum seekers and refugees.

Eileen Pittaway, PhD, is Director of the Centre for Refugee Research, University of New South Wales, Sydney, Australia, and teaches in the School of Social Sciences, in the Master Programs of International Social Development, and Refugees and Forced Migration. She has conducted research, acted as technical advisor and evaluated humanitarian and development projects around the world. A major focus of her work is the ethics of research with vulnerable populations, with a focus on refugees and migrants. A key outcome of her work with Linda Bartolomei was significant input into the drafting and acceptance of a new United Nations Economic and Social Council Conclusion (soft international law) on the protection of women and girls at risk.

Elisha Riggs is a postdoctoral research fellow at the Murdoch Children's Research Institute. With a background in public health and health promotion, she completed her PhD at the University of Melbourne. She has considerable research experience in refugee and migrant child health inequalities, social determinants of health, ethics, partnerships, mixed methods intervention implementation and evaluation. Her research utilises participatory and culturally competent methodologies in partnership with culturally diverse communities. She has published on topics including refugee access and engagement with health services (*BMC Health Services Research, Global Health Promotion*), cultural competence in public health research (*Encyclopaedia of Public Health*) and ethical considerations in qualitative research (*Monash Bioethics Review*).

Deborah Zion is a senior lecturer at the International Public Health unit, School of Public Health and Preventive Medicine at Monash University. She received her PhD in 2001 in Human Bioethics and has published widely on issues related to research with vulnerable populations, refugee health and the ethics of care for asylum seekers. In 2007 she received an Australian Research Council grant, with Linda Briskman and Bebe Loff, entitled 'Caring for Asylum Seekers in Australia. Bioethics and Human Rights'. Her chapter in this volume forms part of that project. She has also published on issues relating to nursing in detention, psychiatry and asylum seekers, and asylum seeker detention as a form of torture.

ACKNOWLEDGEMENTS

This book is the result of a collaborative effort for which many people deserve our recognition and gratitude. It grew out of a symposium on the same topic, which was conceptualised and organised by Researchers for Asylum Seekers, a group of the University of Melbourne academics and associates who aim to promote the humane treatment of asylum seekers and refugees. Particular thanks go to Nikola Balvin, Karmen Jobling, Joanne Tropea, Dean Lusher and Surjeet Dhanji for their enthusiasm, support and assistance with this event. We would like to express our appreciation also to the large number of people who attended. Firstly, their enthusiasm and interest confirmed that there was both a need and an audience for a volume such as this; and secondly, their participation in the vigorous discussions that accompanied the day's presentations, doubtlessly contributed much to the contributions that ultimately appear here. We are especially grateful to all of our contributors, who include those who presented at the symposium and a number of additional scholars. Their immediate willingness to commit to this project and dedicate their time, wisdom and insights brought the book to fruition. Additional thanks go to the McCaughey Centre, The University of Melbourne for its financial support for both the symposium and the book; and to our families, colleagues and friends whose support and encouragement were invaluable. Finally, we would like to dedicate the book to those current and former refugees and asylum seekers, whose wellbeing is the ultimate aim of the research that this volume would guide.

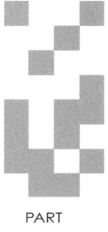

PART

1

ETHICAL FRAMEWORKS
AND
KEY CONCEPTS

CHAPTER

1

Ethics in Research With Refugees and Asylum Seekers: Processes, Power and Politics

Karen Block, Elisha Riggs, and Nick Haslam

Forced migration is a growing global issue. The United Nations High Commissioner for Refugees (UNHCR) listed the number of 'people of concern' — comprising refugees, internally displaced persons, asylum seekers and stateless people — at approximately 20 million in 2000, expanding to approximately 34 million people a decade later (UNHCR, 2012). While the majority of the world's refugees flee *from*, and *to*, less developed countries, the number of asylum claims in wealthy industrialised countries is also rising.

Accompanying this escalation in the number of forcibly displaced people is a corresponding growth in the demand for research. Systematic inquiries are needed to understand and improve the circumstances in which refugees live, and to guide national and international policies and programs. Researchers working in this area are invariably committed to social justice, the corollary of which is a close connection between refugee scholarship and advocacy. It is also clearly imperative that scholars working in this field must *first, do no harm*. However, there are many ethical complications in conducting research with uprooted people, who have often been exposed to persecution and marginalisation in conflict situations, refugee camps, immigration detention settings, and following resettlement. Moreover, these complications arise throughout the research process, from formulating a question through to the dissemination of findings.

Ethical challenges for researchers who seek to understand refugee experiences also frequently have methodological implications. They include the process of negotiating access to research participants and obtaining informed consent; the sensitivities involved in gaining and respecting the trust of participants; the logistics of working with different language groups, varying literacy levels and diverse understandings of research; the imbalance of power between researchers and participants; and the need to maximise inclusion and agency in the research process. The highly charged political environment in which much refugee research takes place adds to this complexity, often creating tensions between rigour and advocacy. Ethical guidelines such as those produced by the Refugee Studies Centre, University of Oxford (Refugee Studies Centre, 2007), set out the general principles for ethical research on forced migration. It is the goal of this collection to explore how such general principles operate in practice and to embed them in a broader intellectual context.

This book grew out of a symposium on the same topic, held at the University of Melbourne in November 2010 organised by the first two editors as representatives of the Researchers for Asylum Seekers group. The symposium brought together key scholars with expertise in refugee and asylum seeker research to discuss the ethical dimensions, challenges and tensions of research conducted with these groups. It attracted widespread interest from researchers, students, members of government departments and the nongovernment sector. Each of the speakers contributed a chapter to this volume as did a number of additional high-profile national and international scholars with established expertise in the ethics of research with refugees and asylum seekers.

The collection is intentionally multidisciplinary — while all the authors are actively engaged in refugee research, their respective disciplines include anthropology, bioethics, public health, criminology, psychology, philosophy, psychiatry, social policy and social work. Previous studies of the ethical issues involved in research with refugees and asylum seekers have been relatively narrow in disciplinary terms. This book is therefore unique, in that it encompasses the theoretical, conceptual, practical, and applied aspects of research ethics, while integrating different disciplinary perspectives. It is intended as a resource not only for researchers, students and practitioners working with refugees and asylum seekers across a broad range of disciplines, but also for those conducting cross-cultural research more broadly. Many of its arguments, examples and concerns are pertinent to research with other vulnerable or marginalised populations.

Ethical Considerations in Research With Refugees and Asylum Seekers

Three fundamental themes recur throughout this book, and other work concerned with the ethics of refugee research: vulnerability, power, and the relationship between research and advocacy. This section will briefly consider each of these recognised ethical challenges, and is followed by an overview of subsequent chapters.

Vulnerability

Vulnerability in research is a contested concept, and one that is almost inevitably an implicit factor when considering the ethics of research with refugees and asylum seekers. In some cases, the vulnerability of these groups is simply assumed. In other cases, this label is resisted as implying a 'deficit-position', which disregards the resilience and agency of those fleeing persecution. Understanding the potential vulnerability of research participants as resulting from the circumstances in which they find themselves — rather than locating it within the person — helps to remind us that such groups consist of 'ordinary people' buffeted by extraordinary — albeit disturbingly common — events.

Historically, the issue of vulnerability in research ethics is associated with groups of people who may have decreased capacity to give informed consent or who have a heightened susceptibility to coercion. Coleman (2009) makes the point that while the concept of vulnerability has 'intuitive ethical appeal', deeming whole *populations* or *categories* of people as vulnerable, lacks sensitivity to context and fails to consider what a person might be vulnerable *to*. One suggestion for addressing this conceptual deficiency is that vulnerability be defined as 'an identifiably increased likelihood of incurring additional or greater wrong' (Hurst, 2008, p. 195). Coleman takes this further, arguing that in relation to research ethics, it is useful to consider three distinct types of vulnerability. The first of these, 'consent-based vulnerability', arises where there are barriers to obtaining meaningfully informed and voluntary consent. The second, 'risk-based vulnerability', entails an enhanced level of research-related risk of harms. The third, 'justice-based vulnerability', arises where neither the individuals participating in a study (who take on the associated risks and inconvenience), nor the society of which they are members, benefit directly from the outcomes of the research. It is not difficult to envisage situations where one or more of these specific vulnerabilities might apply to refugees and asylum seekers involved in research.

Power

One of the circumstances that may render refugees and asylum seekers vulnerable is a relative lack of power. Given that abuse of power is often the precondition for people becoming refugees in the first place, it is not surprising that a key ethical concern for a number of researchers is the disparity in power between researchers and researched. Such disparities leave the disempowered 'subject' susceptible to harms through misrepresentation by researchers or misuse of findings. Reflexive practice along with collaborative and participatory methods may alleviate some of these risks (Block, Warr, Gibbs, & Riggs, 2013; Ellis, Kia-Keating, Yusuf, Lincoln, & Nur, 2007; Goodnow, in press; Pittaway, Bartolomei, & Hugman, 2010). Participatory approaches to research, by drawing on the direct experiences and knowledge of its intended beneficiaries, are considered more likely to produce relevant knowledge for informing policies and practices. 'A participatory world view' also implies an ethics of emancipation, human rights and equality (Swartz, 2011). However, Doná (2007) warns against easy assumptions that 'participatory' research is of itself an 'empowering' experience for refugee participants, if it fails to advocate for transformation and challenge the disempowering social and political conditions that they face.

Power asymmetries pose particular challenges for negotiating appropriately informed consent (Ellis et al., 2007; Mackenzie, McDowell, & Pittaway, 2007; Pittaway et al., 2010). Ellis and colleagues suggest that the very notion of informed and voluntary consent may have little relevance in some contexts, given that the constructs it invokes assume 'culturally bound, western values of individual autonomy, self-determination, and freedom' (Ellis et al., 2007, p. 467). It is critical therefore, that consent be seen as a process that includes ongoing negotiation over involvement in the research process and development of authentic understanding of what the research requires (Mackenzie et al., 2007).

The cross-cultural nature of most refugee research raises additional methodological and ethical concerns that implicate power. Birman (2006) makes the point that ethical behaviour may be defined differently within different cultures, and any imposition of dominant concepts and measures that originate in the researchers' culture may therefore misrepresent the phenomena of interest. Emphasising the interdependence of methods, scientific validity and ethics, several writers have argued for caution when attempting to use standardised research instruments and techniques that may be inaccurate or inappropriate for different cultural groups or attempting to measure constructs that do not exist or have different meanings in different cultures (Birman & Chan, 2008; Ellis et al., 2007).

Research and/or Advocacy

Issues of vulnerability and power pervade the relationship between the researcher and the researched, and the obligations that the former owe the latter. This leads many researchers to adopt an explicitly political stance that views research as a tool for advocacy. Many would argue further, that to stop short of such a position, and regard research as a neutral quest for knowledge, risks inflicting harm. In environments where refugees are rendered particularly vulnerable — such as when lacking legal recognition by states or living in unsafe camp conditions for example — there is a very real risk that mishandled information obtained through research could further compromise their safety (Mackenzie et al., 2007). In some cases, researchers need to anticipate ways in which their mere presence may be construed as a political act. Using the treatment of asylum seekers in Australian detention centres as an example, Zion and colleagues (2010) have argued that research conducted under such conditions — where gaining access to research participants necessarily involves negotiating an agreement between researchers and responsible authorities — may risk lending legitimacy to pathological systems. In response to these concerns, others have made the point that *failing* to engage asylum seekers in research into their conditions, may constitute a further assault on their agency and autonomy (Bloom, 2010; Rousseau & Kirmayer, 2010). Moreover, addressing this risk of complicity — and echoing Doná's position that researchers should aim for transformative participation — Rousseau and Kirmayer (2010) assert that:

> Research ethics ... require a firm commitment to advocacy. No matter how carefully and respectfully information is collected, if it is not coupled with vigorous efforts to use it to transform the situation of ongoing violence, then the weight of complicity may be too much to bear. (p. 66)

However, a position of overt solidarity between researcher and researched is not without critics. Jacobsen and Landau (2003) contend that a tendency towards 'advocacy research' in refugee and humanitarian studies frequently results in a lack of research rigour, 'where researchers already know what they want to see and say, and come away from the research having 'proved' it' (p. 187). Critical of qualitative approaches in particular, they argue that much of this research is subjective and methodologically flawed, and therefore has limited academic credibility and ability to inform policy appropriately. Research based on unsound methodology is, they argue, by its nature ethically suspect and may lead directly to harms when its findings are (mis)applied (Jacobsen & Landau, 2003, p. 190). Notwithstanding these assertions, and endorsing the importance of a rigorous methodological approach, the more common perspective is that 'in refugee studies, scholarship is embedded in advocacy and advocacy in scholarship' (Voutira & Dona, 2007, p. 167). Taking this position further, Mackenzie and colleagues (2007) maintain that where researchers are in a position to intervene on the behalf of research participants in need, failure to do so, in the name of scholarly objectivity, is itself an unethical stance (Mackenzie et al., 2007). Arguing for an ethics that goes beyond harm minimisation to one of reciprocity, they suggest that to do less can turn research into an exploitative process, the main outcome of which is a furthering of the researchers' careers.

Overview of this Volume

It is clear, even from this brief discussion, that conducting research with refugees and other displaced persons is a necessity that presents researchers with a number of ethical dilemmas. Again drawing on the example of research into Australia's immigration detention system, Justo (2010) graphically describes the challenge. Arguing for the importance of conducting such research, he observes that 'as to how should it be done, researchers will have to thread a narrow strait between the Scylla of silence and the Charybdis of endangering refugees' conditions' (p. 62). It is anticipated that this book will assist researchers in that task.

The following chapters are divided into three distinct sections. The first section discusses a range of ethical frameworks for conducting research with refugees and asylum seekers; the second focuses on ethical research methodologies; the third examines the ethical implications of research in relation to advocacy, and its influence on policy and politics.

Part 1: Ethical Frameworks and Key Concepts

Each of the chapters in this section reflects on an ethical framework, key concept or lens that informs the design and planning of research. It begins with a discussion of the role of formal ethical requirements and frameworks in shaping refugee research. Moving from explicit formal guidelines to implicit understandings, the second chapter examines the discrepant 'value cultures' that researchers, research participants, institutional ethics committees and other stakeholders bring to their conceptualisation of refugees, the research process and one another. This is followed up by a third chapter that analyses the role of potentially misplaced assumptions of vulnerability that influence researchers and research ethics committee. The fourth chapter in this section deals with another key conceptual lens — the impact of power gradients on the ethics of refugee research — contrasting the differing position of the researcher with respect to policy-makers and to refugee participants.

In chapter 2, Lynn Gillam, an ethicist with a background in philosophy, examines the utility and limitations of formal ethical guidelines for researchers working with refugee and asylum seeker populations. Focusing on Australia's *National Statement on Ethical Conduct in Human Research* (National Statement) in particular, she suggests that such frameworks offer useful general guidance but still leave much room for interpretation. Leaving aside a number of important ethical decisions, including what research should be conducted and how findings should be used, the National Statement concentrates firstly on whether a particular research proposal should proceed and secondly on the processes of conducting research. Operationalising core ethical principles of research merit and integrity, respect for human beings, justice, and beneficence, it directs researchers, and ethics review committees, to attend to the balance between risks and benefits of research participation, and whether consent is likely to be genuinely informed and voluntary. In order to aid the process of appropriate ethical review of research proposals involving refugees and asylum seekers, Gillam advises that researchers should include in their projects, an investigation of the experiences that their participants have of research participation and publish these findings.

Sandy Gifford's chapter explores the idea of 'value cultures' as a way to apprehend 'fields of difference' in refugee research. Noting that conflicts commonly arise between researchers, ethics committees, service providers and refugees themselves over the nature and desirability of research, Gifford argues that these tensions spring in part from discrepant values and understandings of what it is to be a refugee. These value cultures shape the identities of the groups involved, give different meanings to the ideals of protecting and not harming refugees, and often result in the erasure of refugee voices. For example, refugees are sometimes 'reduced to a collective identity woven around notions of persecution, vulnerability, dependency and need'. This reductive view, which is linked to a well-meaning desire to protect refugees from the perceived dangers of research, denies them individuality, autonomy and agency, and binds them to a single identity that obliterates all others. The chapter uses an anthropologist's conceptual tools to expose the roots of contestation over the nature of research ethics in the field of refugee studies. In the process it offers hopes that interested parties in the research process can come to comprehend one another's diverging views and reach some common ground.

In the following chapter, Christopher McDowell interrogates the construction by ethics review committees of displaced people as occupying a category of vulnerability, and the implications this has in terms of understandings of autonomy, agency and responsibility. He argues that a particular type of 'refugeeness' — based on a refugee camp paradigm, where a refugee is characterised by extreme vulnerability, a 'lack of power, autonomy, and dignity, and occupies a liminal political space' — has been projected onto other displaced populations such as those fleeing deteriorating environmental conditions and poverty. Researchers (and NGOs), cognisant of the structural disadvantages leading to dislocation, are likely to be complicit in this conflation of different categories of displacement as conferring vulnerability. However this lumping together of different categories ignores the complexity of contemporary migration flows, disregards the agency demonstrated during other types of forced migration and reduces capacity for investigating and understanding the actual experiences of these groups. McDowell, a political scientist, therefore urges researchers and review committees to disaggregate displacement, and consider separately the ethical implications of differences in autonomy, vulnerability, access to state protection and capacity to engage in political action typically experienced by conflict refugees, asylum seekers, 'environmental refugees' and 'development refugees'.

In the final chapter of this section, Marinella Marmo delves into the complexities of power relations when researchers conduct research with refugees in 'crisis conditions', using as an example, the situation of asylum seekers in detention centres. Drawing on her background as a criminologist, she prefaces this investigation with a discussion of the paradoxical status of the refugee as 'victim-offender'. This position is ascribed to asylum seekers by governments and some sections of the media, who demonstrate a neo-liberal stance deeming asylum seekers responsible for their own victim status, thereby losing their image as 'idealised' defenceless and passive victims through taking action. They further 'offend' through projected complicity with people smugglers. The social researcher thus enters a highly politicised field, usually identifying the asylum seeker as the voiceless sufferer whose voice he/she aims to become. Marmo argues that the fundamental job of the researcher is to generate knowledge, and questions the ethical propriety of turning research into direct social activism, particularly where research participants believe there will be a direct benefit to them from the research. She anchors this argument in an examination of the difference between the way power operates at the macro (political) level and the micro (interpersonal) level within refugee research. At a macro level, the researcher is attempting to disrupt the malign influences of power on refugees' lives and the narratives shaping their representation as deviant offender. This is fundamentally an ethical undertaking, which aims to reduce harms and promote justice. At a micro (personal) level, however, the researcher is in a dominant position with respect to the asylum seeker. This creates ethical complications, with postcolonial overtones, as the researcher — who usually represents an ethnically or socially privileged group - dominates and represents the 'voiceless' research subject. Marmo concludes by suggesting that participatory models of research *may* redress this power imbalance and that these need to be systematically evaluated using power as an ethical lens.

Part 2: Methodological Approaches to Ethical Research

This section concentrates on the nexus between research ethics and the use of appropriate methodologies. Its chapters consider both the guiding principles and the mechanics of research, speaking directly to the ethical tensions that arise when recruiting research participants and obtaining informed consent, and exploring the ethical implications of using a range of methods and approaches.

The first chapter in this section by psychologists Jeanette Lawrence, Ida Kaplan and Colleen McFarlane, focuses on respect as a guiding principle for researcher interactions with children and adolescents from refugee backgrounds. While acknowledging problems with applying the concept of vulnerability to a whole group such as refugee young people, they recognise that the refugee experience is likely to leave young refugees at risk of incurring additional harms associated with research. Making a case, nonetheless, for including refugee young people in research, the authors argue that this additional risk of harm does not require a response of 'prohibitive protectionism'; rather it calls for the considered application of the principle of respect. They distinguish between three forms of respect: universal respect due to all persons; protective respect due to those who have suffered; and beneficial or compensatory respect. They also note the potential for research conducted in this way to have a positive psychological impact on participants whose previous experiences have denied them respect. There are several 'decision points' in a research project where respect needs to be applied, and these include aligning methods, instruments and procedures with the interests and experiences of participants.

Hariz Halilovich, in the next chapter, argues for the interconnectedness between methodology and ethics in refugee research. He contends that ultimately researchers need to engage actively in advancing the human rights of their participants in order to link the questions of how we do research with refugees and why we do it. Drawing on examples from his own anthropological research as 'a cultural insider' with displaced people from Bosnia Herzegovina, he proposes participatory action research as one way of actively achieving this link, due to its focus on empowerment of participants through both the *processes* and the *outcomes*. He describes how he used focus groups as a way to bring socially isolated adolescents and women together to address their isolation and facilitate their collaboration in addressing common issues, thus blurring the distinction between research and intervention. Entering the debate over objectivity versus partisanship, Halilovich argues that the ethical obligations to participants mean that 'refugee research can never be apolitical or 'objectively neutral".

In the third chapter of this section, Eileen Pittaway and Linda Bartolomei, with backgrounds in social policy and social work, also describe a research model based on the principles of participatory action research as providing the ethical basis for their work. They describe their methodology — 'Reciprocal Research', or 'Community Consultation' — as an interactive and evolving process, which involves providing training and working collaboratively with refugee women to address problems the women themselves have identified. The methodology is based on the premise that all people have capabilities and the capacity to address community problems if the resources are made available. The aim of this approach is 'to influence change at a legal, policy and service provision level, and to respect the inherent rights and dignity, knowledge and skills of research participants'. It thus explicitly makes the link between ethical and rigorous methodologies and research outcomes including advocacy, which is the subject of the next section.

Part 3: Advocacy and Politics — Considering the Ramifications of Research

This section develops this theme of advocacy further, focusing on the impact and potential repercussions of research. Chapters in this section consider ways in which research findings may be used and abused within a politicised research environment and the inherent ethical tensions that arise when conducting 'policy-relevant' research with a 'vulnerable' population. The final chapter concludes with the assertion that the core ethical principles, which underpin the previous chapters, can ultimately be reduced to the demand that the researcher enacts their responsibility to those they research.

The first chapter in this section, by psychiatrist Louise Newman, reviews the ethical dilemmas of researchers and researcher clinicians working within Australia's immigration detention system. In this deeply politicised context, where government rhetoric characterised protest behaviour as manipulative rather than driven by desperation and distress, there was, and remains, a vital need for researchers to study and document the harm caused by this system to the mental health of detainees. This need raises a number of ethical challenges involving the boundaries between research, advocacy and personal involvement. Working within a detention environment, which itself is the major cause of distress, problematises the whole psychological approach of individual diagnosis and treatment of mental health problems. Nonetheless, clinical research has played a critical role in bringing to light the damage caused by the detention system and the need for reform. Thus clinical work becomes inextricably linked with research (by documenting harms), and advocacy. Ethical dilemmas arise, however, because research and advocacy roles are driven by, but also potentially conflict with, the need to provide care for vulnerable clients.

The ethicist Deborah Zion also draws on experiences of conducting research within harsh and remote centres that form the Australian detention system. Her chapter considers ethical issues that arise when researchers hear stigmatising and dangerous information in the context of government and media rhetoric that already stigmatises and belittles asylum seekers. Using as an example the demonstration of social suffering and mental distress evidenced by described misuse of prescription painkillers, she discusses the additional ethical complication that this was 'nonpartici-pant' information supplied by health care practitioners rather than the asylum seekers themselves, about whom information was given without their consent. In this example, a decision had been made by researchers not to interview asylum seekers directly, because of complications in obtaining genuinely informed consent. While interviewing relatively 'empowered' health care providers instead thus resolved one ethical problem, it also created another. It pro-tected asylum seekers from potential harms of the *processes* of research but not from the potential harms of *publication of the results* even long after the research was completed. This example emphasises the potential for ethical dilemmas to arise when the ethical imperative to report conflicts with an ethical imperative to protect those being researched.

In the final chapter, Mammad Aidani, an interdisciplinary scholar with a background in sociolinguistics, philosophy, litera-ture, and psychology reflects on his research with Iranian refugees who have settled in Australia, which focused on their experiences of displacement, trauma and postdisplacement construction of identity. He bases his discussion on the philosophical work of French phenomenologist Emmanuel Levinas, which underscores responsibility to the 'other' as the central concern of ethics. Using this fundamental insight, Aidani asks, 'what is the responsibility of the researcher to the participant? How is responsibility towards the participant enacted?' He concludes that the implication of this notion of ethical responsibility demands that the researcher recog-nises refugee research as a political act; and responds with not only compassion but also a commitment to social justice.

Conclusion

This returns us to our contention at the beginning of this chapter, that it is this very commitment to the promotion of justice, which often provides the motivation for research with refugees and asylum seekers in the first place. This commitment throws into sharp relief, the fundamental challenges and dilemmas encountered in research with respect to this and to other core ethical principles — of respect for persons and concern for their welfare. We have suggested here that these challenges generally revolve around predicaments involving vulnerability, power, advocacy and the political ramifications of research.

The chapters in this volume bring together the collective and multidisciplinary insights of experienced researchers into how they have negotiated these predicaments. While in many cases, these insights and experiences draw attention to additional questions, rather than provide definitive answers, they nonetheless provide invaluable guidance as to how researchers in the field may operationalise guiding principles. Perhaps the overriding message is the need for researchers to consider carefully the context-dependant and contingent nature of their enterprise and to balance vigilantly issues of vulnerability, respect and responsibility.

References

Birman, D. (2006). Ethical issues in research with immigrants and refugees. In J.E. Trimble & C.B. Fisher (Eds.), *The handbook of ethical research with ethnocultural populations and communities* (pp.155–177). Thousand Oaks, CA: Sage.

Block, K., Warr, D., Gibbs, L., & Riggs, E. (2013). Addressing ethical and methodological challenges in research with refugee-background young people: Reflections from the field. *Journal of Refugee Studies, 26*(1), 69–87.

Bloom, T. (2010). Asylum seekers: Subjects or objects of research? *The American Journal of Bioethics, 10*(2), 59–60.

Coleman, C.H. (2009). Vulnerability as a regulatory category in human subject research. *The Journal of Law, Medicine & Ethics, 37*(1), 12–18.

Doná, G. (2007). The microphysics of participation in refugee research. *Journal of Refugee Studies, 20*(2), 210–229.

Ellis, B.H., Kia-Keating, M., Yusuf, S.A., Lincoln, A., & Nur, A. (2007). Ethical research in refugee communities and the use of community participatory methods. *Transcultural Psychiatry, 44*(3), 459–481.

Goodnow, J. (in press). Refugees, asylum-seekers, displaced persons: Children in precarious positions. In A. Ben-Arieh, J. Cashmore, G. Goodman, & G. Melton (Eds.), *Handbook of child research.* New York, NY: Sage.

Hurst, S.A. (2008). Vulnerability in research and health care; describing the elephant in the room? *Bioethics, 22*(4), 191–202.

Jacobsen, K., & Landau, L.B. (2003). The dual imperative in refugee research: Some methodological and ethical considerations in social science research on forced migration. *Disasters, 27*(3), 185–206.

Justo, L. (2010). Consent while hanging from a cliff? *The American Journal of Bioethics, 10*(2), 61–62.

Mackenzie, C., McDowell, C., & Pittaway, E. (2007). Beyond 'Do no harm': The challenge of constructing ethical relationships in refugee research. *Journal of Refugee Studies, 20*(2), 299–319.

Pittaway, E., Bartolomei, L., & Hugman, R. (2010). 'Stop stealing our stories': The ethics of research with vulnerable groups. *Journal of Human Rights Practice, 2*(2), 229–251.

Refugee Studies Centre. (2007). Ethical guidelines for good research practice. *Refugee Survey Quarterly, 26*(3), 162–172.

Rousseau, C., & Kirmayer, L.J. (2010). From complicity to advocacy: The necessity of refugee research. *The American Journal of Bioethics, 10*(2), 65–67.

Swartz, S. (2011). 'Going deep' and 'giving back': Strategies for exceeding ethical expectations when researching amongst vulnerable youth. *Qualitative Research, 11*(1), 47–68.

United Nations High Commissioner for Refugees (UNHCR). (2012). Statistical Online Population Database. Retrieved from http://www.unhcr.org/pages/4a013eb06.html

Voutira, E., & Dona, G. (2007). Refugee research methodologies: Consolidation and transformation of a field. *Journal of Refugee Studies, 20*(2), 163–171.

Zion, D., Briskman, L., & Loff, B. (2010). Returning to history: The ethics of researching asylum seeker health in Australia. *The American Journal of Bioethics, 10*(2), 48–56.

CHAPTER

2

Ethical Considerations in Refugee Research: What Guidance Do Formal Research Ethics Documents Offer?

Lynn Gillam

Research with refugees and asylum seekers is conducted in an ethically fraught context. Fundamental aspects of human rights and international law are at stake, as well as the ultimate ethical question of what obligation of beneficence human beings owe to each other. On top of this, the debate about asylum seekers and refugees around the world is highly politicised and highly emotive. These are tricky waters for researchers to navigate, but they may be the very waters that they feel morally or professionally compelled to enter.

One place that researchers may look to for guidance is the formal human research ethics framework. This includes international statements of ethical principles in human research, notably the World Medical Association's *Declaration of Helsinki* and the *International Ethical Guidelines for Biomedical Research Involving Human Subjects,* issued by the Council for International Organisations of Medical Science and the World Health Organization, as well as the national documents of many countries that set our requirements for formal ethical review of research involving humans, and ethical standards that research must meet in order to receive approval. In Australia, the ethics review process requires that all research conducted under the auspices of publicly funded research institutions, including universities, research institutes and public hospitals, must be approved by a properly constituted human research ethics committee (HREC). This is a condition under which public monies are provided for research through the major funding bodies, the National Health and Medical Research Council (NHMRC), and the Australian Research Council (ARC). The requirement applies not only to medical research, but also to any research of any nature that involves human participants. The key document, which sets out the role and functions of HRECs and the ethical principles to which research should conform, is the National Health and Medical Research Council (NHMRC, 2007, updated 2009) *National Statement on Ethical Conduct in Human Research* (the 'National Statement').

In this chapter, I will consider what sort of guidance is given for research involving refugees and asylum seekers in the National Statement. I will show that some useful guidance is given on the matter of what constitutes ethical practice in the conduct of research in this field, but that there is still considerable room for interpretation in relation to individual studies. I will suggest that HRECs are not necessarily well equipped with the appropriate knowledge and experience to meaningfully carry out this inter-pretation for refugee or asylum seeker research. While this analy-sis is based on the text of the Australian National Statement, the same sort of conclusion would be reached by a similar analysis of the research ethics guidelines of other countries (such as the United States [US] 'Common Rule', which is the federal policy on protection for human research subjects; and the Canadian Tri-Council *Policy Statement on Ethical Conduct for Research Involving Humans*), many of which give guidance which is even less specific in relation to refugee research than that provided in the National Statement.

I will also argue that researchers who work in this field can and should be involved in assisting in this task. Research ethics is most fruitfully seen as a collaborative enterprise, in which researchers and research ethics committees work together to produce research of a high ethical standard. Researchers have an important role to play in this process. This role includes investigation of the experiences that their participants have of research participation, and the impacts it has on them. This material needs to be published and made available to research ethics committees, along with other published evidence of the effects of research participation on asylum seekers and refugees. There is also arguably a role for an organisation or professional body of researchers in this field to promote and coordinate such research, and to use the findings to develop some agreed standards and practices for ethical research with refugees and asylum seekers.

Some Ethical Questions About Refugee Research

There are many questions that could be asked in relation to the ethics of refugee and asylum seeker research. Here are four:

(1) Is there an ethical obligation to conduct research with refugees and asylum seekers, to determine what impact policies in this area are having on those who are subject to them?

(2) Is there an ethical imperative to act on the findings of refugee and asylum seeker research (in particular ways)?

(3) Is it ever ethically appropriate to conduct research with people in such a vulnerable situation, especially those who are detained or involved in legal proceedings?

(4) What are ethically appropriate ways of conducting refugee research?

The first two of these questions are not considered by HRECs, nor does the National Statement provide any guidance on them, even though ethicists and researchers in the field have been very much concerned with them (Johnston, 2009; McNeill, 2003; Zion, Briskman, & Loff, 2010). HRECs do not consider broader ethical questions of what research should be done or prioritised, and how research findings should be used. The National Statement gives only the most general and indirect guidance about such matters and even that has to be inferred from what is said about the core ethical principles for human research (see later). Following this lead, the focus of a HREC is on *internal* ethical aspects of research; that is, how a particular proposed research study will be conducted. The way in which institutions have framed the role and functions of HREC supports this focus. HRECs have become firmly embedded in the research governance processes of institutions. They have a large workload of applications for ethics approval, and their primary task is to get through this workload in a timely fashion. Research-intensive institutions depend on their HRECs to be effective and efficient in this primary task, so that research is not unduly delayed. Realistically, HRECs do not have time to consider the bigger picture questions which particular ethics applications sometimes raise, nor do their institutions typically ask them to do. This is not because HREC members do not see these issues or do not care about them, but on the whole they are beyond the HREC's perceived remit. If research institutions do consider questions of what research is prioritised, or how research findings should be taken up and acted upon, they do so through other mechanisms.

For these reasons, then, it is only the last two of the four questions outlined earlier that the National Statement and HRECs can provide any meaningful guidance on, specifically, (3) whether it is ever ethically appropriate to conduct research involving refugees and asylum seekers, and (4) how to conduct such research in ethically appropriate ways. These can be thought of as the 'whether' and 'how' questions, respectively. In the following sections, I will set out the key sections of the National Statement that help to answer these two questions.

Core Ethical Principles as Stated in the National Statement

The National Statement identifies four basic ethical principles for research involving human beings. These principles are: research merit and integrity, respect for human beings, justice, and beneficence (see section 1, p. 11). These principles are standard in the field of research ethics. They are very similar to those articulated or implied in the research ethics guidelines of many other countries (e.g., US, United Kingdom [UK], Canada), and international codes of research ethics (e.g., Declaration of Helsinki, Council for International Organizations of Medical Sciences). They can ultimately be traced back to the influential Belmont Report (1979), the report of The National Commission for the Protection of Human Subjects of Biomedical and Behavioral Research, which first set out the general ethical principles for human research in this style. The ethical principles set out in the National Statement are intended to guide both researchers and HREC members. They give a good general indication of what HRECs will be looking for when they review a research proposal of any kind. What they might specifically indicate for refugee and asylum seeker research is discussed below.

Scientific Merit and Integrity

The National Statement frames the merit of the research and the integrity of researchers as the cornerstone requirements for ethical research: 'Unless proposed research has merit, and the researchers who are to carry out the research have integrity, the involvement of human participants in the research cannot be ethically justifiable' (section 1, p. 11). 'Merit' has a specific meaning in this context. It is not enough that the research is well intentioned, or motivated by concern for social justice or human rights. The research must have specific aims, which are worthwhile, and must be well designed in terms of methodology, so that those aims are capable of being achieved (see section 1.1[a)] and [b], p. 12). One important implication in relation to refugee and asylum seeker research is that the aims need to be realistic, otherwise they are not achievable. For political and social reasons alone, the situation of refugees and asylum seekers will not easily or quickly be changed. Particular research studies may realistically aim to provide evidence, which could feed into policy development or improvement in service delivery, or to evaluate the effects of an intervention or program, but it is not realistic for one study to aim to transform the situation of all asylum seekers or refugees. The idea of researcher integrity is explained as involving the honest conduct of research, according to recognised principles of researcher conduct and 'disseminating and communicating results, whether favourable or unfavourable, in ways that permit scrutiny and contribute to public knowledge and understanding' (see section 1.3, p. 12). This last aspect is perhaps particularly pertinent to asylum seeker research, if researchers are working in a situation where there may be pressure placed on them to limit disclosure of their research findings, or to shape their findings in a particular way. In each case, researchers need to consider whether the research context will actually allow them to conduct their research with integrity. If not, then it may be necessary to conclude that the answer to the 'whether' question is 'no'; that is, it would not be ethical to conduct that particular research in that particular setting. This conclusion might be reached if, for example, researchers were to be allowed access to an immigration detention facility only on condition that their findings could only be published if the governing agency approved of them. However, if full freedom of publication were allowed, then the same research project could be conducted with integrity and would be ethical to undertake.

Respect for Human Beings (Autonomy and Informed Consent)

The National Statement accords high value to respect for human beings:

> Among these values, respect is central. It involves recognising that each human being has value in himself or herself, and that this value must inform all interaction between people. Such respect includes recognising the value of human autonomy — the capacity to determine one's own life and make one's own decisions. But respect goes further than this. It also involves providing for the protection of those with diminished or no autonomy, as well as empowering them where possible and protecting and helping people wherever it would be wrong not to do so. (section 1, p. 11)

These words are a powerful expression of the meaning and importance of respect for human beings. Indeed, they may resonate with researchers in the field as articulating the very reasons that they have embarked upon research with refugees and asylum seekers in the first place. These words may suggest that the answer to the 'whether' question about ethical appropriateness question is a resounding 'yes', provided of course that the process for conducting the research also accords with the value of respect. On the other hand, these words may perhaps give pause — for example, immigration detention centres remove autonomy of those detained, and researchers need to question whether it is possible to conduct research that respects autonomy in a setting which does not respect autonomy. One way of addressing this issue is to consider what is required for informed consent. This is because informed consent is the major practical mechanism for putting into practice the principle of respect for autonomy. The National Statement provides some specific guidance on what constitutes informed consent:

> The guiding principle for researchers is that a person's decision to participate in research is to be voluntary, and based on sufficient information and adequate understanding of both the pro-

posed research and the implications of participation in it. (section 2.2.1, p. 19)

There are two key components of informed consent — adequate understanding and voluntariness. Both of these can be problematic for refugee and asylum seeker research. Adequate understanding, according to the National Statement, involves 'an adequate understanding of the purpose, methods, demands, risks and potential benefits of the research' (section 2.2.2, p. 19). One challenge, perhaps the most well recognised, is how to mitigate the effects of cultural and language difference to convey all of the information in a way that makes it genuinely understandable. A more subtle concern is that the way in which asylum seekers and refugees are approached to participate in research may lead them to misinterpret risks and benefits. If people overestimate the possible risks, due to fear, anxiety, feelings of vulnerability, or mistrust of authorities, then this is not a major ethical problem, provided that they feel able to say 'no'. They simply decline to participate, and there are no further consequences for them (as the National Statement requires [at section 4.3.7, p. 60] 'persons declining to participate should not suffer any negative consequences'). However, if people underestimate risks, or overestimate the potential benefits to them, this does have serious ethical implications. In this case, people may agree to participate in research because they incorrectly perceive that it is likely to bring benefits to them (here, the imagined benefits may include granting of refugee status, granting of immigration visas to family members, release from detention, a job, better housing, and more). If the risks are under estimated at the same time, the situation is ethically even worse. People who agree to participate in these circumstances have not really given valid informed consent, no matter how much researchers have tried to convey realistic messages about potential risk and benefit. When the expected or hoped-for benefits do not materialise, participants may feel angry, distressed, betrayed or misused. The National Statement identifies this potential problem. In the section on 'participants in dependent relationships', it points out that 'researchers need to be mindful that in some relationships of dependency, participants may have an unrealistic expectation of the benefits of research' (see section 4.3.6, p. 60).

This poses a challenge for researchers seeking to work with refugees or asylum seekers. If their proposed research may create unrealistic expectation of benefits, researchers must consider how these expectations can be damped down. This is one aspect of the ethical 'how' question outlined at the start. How could the research be designed and conducted to deal with this ethical challenge: What measures could be put in place, and how successful might they be? The National Statement does not offer any specific guidance on what might be done before or during the informed consent process in this regard, although it does implicitly give researchers licence to be quite pro-active and innovative in negotiating informed consent. For example, it notes that informed consent should not be seen as satisfying a formal requirement, but rather as a process aimed at 'mutual understanding between researchers and participants' (see section 2.2.4, p. 19). Expression of consent does not have to be written; it could be done by other means, depending on 'the nature and complexity of the research' and 'the participant's personal and cultural circumstances' (see section 2.2.5, p. 19). So there is considerable room for researchers to work towards resolving the problems of unrealistic expectations of benefit, but it must still be acknowledged that there are limits to what researchers can achieve, when the participants' circumstances are outside the researchers' control. In some situations, the 'whether' question will raise its head. If there are likely to be unrealistic expectations of major benefits, and it is difficult to see how these can be effectively lowered, the question of

whether it is ethically acceptable to conduct research in this situation must be seriously considered. The answer may be 'no'.

Voluntariness, the second key component of informed
consent, is another potentially problematic issue for refugee and
asylum seeker research. The difficulty again is perceptions,
because of the context in which asylum seeker researcher in particular is carried out. As section 2.2.9 of the National Statement
makes clear, voluntariness can be undermined if prospective participants *perceive* researchers to be in a position of power, even if
they are actually not. This problem is not necessarily overcome by
explanations and assurances that potential participants are totally
free to decide against participating in the research, or that neither
the researchers nor the authorities to which the potential participants are subject have any power to compel them to participate,
or to punish or disadvantage them in any way for not participating. Potential participants may feel that they have no choice but
to agree, even if this feeling is unfounded. The National Statement
acknowledges that an unequal or dependent relationship does not
always make consent invalid, but 'it always constitutes a reason to
pay particular attention to the process through which consent is
negotiated' (see section 4.3.1, p. 59). It suggests mechanisms for
ameliorating any sense of coercion:

> researchers should wherever possible invite potential partici-
> pants to discuss their participation with someone who is able to
> support them in making their decision. Where potential partic-
> ipants are especially vulnerable or powerless, consideration
> should be given to the appointment of a participant advocate.
> (section 4.3.2, p. 59)

Nevertheless, the 'whether' question is still lurking. Such mechanisms may not work in resolving this question. If there are likely
to be perceptions of power and coercion, and it will be very difficult to effectively counter these, serious consideration needs to
be given to whether it is ethically appropriate even to attempt
the research in this setting.

Justice

On the ethical principle of justice and its application to human research, the National Statement (2007; updated 2009) has this to say:

> At a profound level, justice involves a regard for the human sameness that each person shares with every other. Human beings have a deep need to be treated in accordance with such justice, which includes distributive justice and procedural justice. In the research context, distributive justice will be expressed in the fair distribution of the benefits and burdens of research, and procedural justice in 'fair treatment' in the recruitment of participants and the review of research. (section 1, p. 11)

There are two aspects of justice that researchers need to take account of in planning, designing and conducting their research. These are distributive justice, and procedural justice (sometimes called 'due process' or 'natural justice'). Note that neither of these aspects of justice refers at all to the big-picture issues of whether policy regimes for refugees or asylum seekers are just, whether individuals are being treated justly in relation to their claims for asylum, whether refugees in the community are being unjustly discriminated against in access to education, housing, or health care. These are questions of justice in the broader sense, but they are not at the focus of the National Statement's guidance on justice in human research. This becomes very clear in the six specific guidelines that are provided in relation to justice. Three of these relate to procedural justice. In research that is 'just':

- taking into account the scope and objectives of the proposed research, the selection, exclusion and inclusion of categories of research participants is fair, and is accurately described in the results of the research
- the process of recruiting participants is fair
- there is no exploitation of participants in the conduct of research (section 1.4, p. 12).

The other three guidelines relate to distributive justice:

- there is no unfair burden of participation in research on particular groups
- there is fair distribution of the benefits of participation in research
- there is fair access to the benefits of research (section 1.4, p. 12).

These last three guidelines prompt researchers to ask whether those who participate in research, or the communities to which they belong, receive a fair share of whatever benefits are generated by research. Or do the benefits go somewhere else. This is a particularly pertinent question when research is conducted on particular groups simply because they are readily accessible, convenient and easy to recruit. Students in universities and staff of research institutions may fall into this category, where, for example, they may end up involved in medical research where the intended benefits are directed entirely towards a different group in the population. This is probably less of a concern for refugees and asylum seeker research, since that research is (mostly, at least) about issues specific to those groups, and the outcomes will be applicable only to those groups. Nevertheless, consideration of the fair distribution of the benefits and burdens of research should prompt questions about whether some groups of refugees are over-researched. It is important to ask whether refugees are sought out as research participants much more frequently than other groups in society, or more frequently than is reasonable given their circumstances. Ethically aware researchers keep in mind that research is intrusive into people's lives, so there must be a good justification for such intrusion. That the researcher is interested or a research student would like to give it a try — these reasons are not in themselves very strong justifications.

Beneficence (and Risk)

According the National Statement:

> Researchers exercise beneficence in several ways: in assessing and taking account of the risks of harm and the potential benefits of research to participants and to the wider community; in being sensitive to the welfare and interests of people involved in their research; and in reflecting on the social and cultural implications of their work. (section 1, p. 11)

This excerpt makes it very clear that risks include, not only physical harm, but also psychological, social, economic and legal harm — and notes that no list of categories of risk can be exhaustive (see section 1, p. 16). The message to researchers is to consider what negative consequences of any sort might foreseeably be caused to participants by their involvement in the research.

Consideration of risks and benefits relates to the ethical 'how' question, and prompts researchers to design and carry out their research in ways that minimise potential risks to the participants, and maximise potential benefits to the participants and the community. The National Statement does not give any specific guidance on types of research design or methods that might be less risky (a sensible silence, since this would be meaningless without taking into account the specifics of each and every research setting). However, it does state a basic obligation to look after the welfare of research participants and to minimise risks to them (see section 1.7, p. 13). It also provides two basic benchmarks. The first relates risks to potential benefits: 'risks to research participants are ethically acceptable only if they are justified by the potential benefits of the research' (see section 2.1.2, p. 17). The second spells out the significance of increasing levels of risk:

> The greater the risks to participants in any research for which ethical approval is given, the more certain it must be both that the risks will be managed as well as possible, and that the participants clearly understand the risks they are assuming. (section 2.1.8, p. 18)

So for researchers working with refugees and asylum seekers, three vital ethical skills, so to speak, are assessing the level of risk, finding ways to carry out research that reduce the risk, as much as possible, and judging the ethical acceptability of the risk that remains. The National Statement spells out the following steps:

- identifying the risks, if any
- assessing the likelihood and severity of the risks
- identifying whom (participants and/or others) the risks may affect
- establishing the means for minimising the risks
- identifying the potential benefits
- identifying to whom benefits are likely to accrue (section 2.1.3, p. 17).

In the field of refugee and asylum seeker research, there is a body of literature about research methods appropriate for the field (e.g., Birman, 2006; Düvell, Triandafyllidou, & Vollmer 2010; Ellis, Kia-Keating, Yusuf, Lincoln, & Nur, 2007; Mackenzie, McDowell, & Pittaway, 2007; Minas, 2004). Responsible researchers will make use of this literature in designing their own research, because it offers both a source of ideas and an evidence base for how best to meet the ethical requirement to minimise risks and maximise benefits.

Ethical principles and the process of human ethics review

Overall, the focus of the National Statement is on risk, benefit and informed consent. This sets for framework for the way that HRECs approach the ethics applications that they receive. Research involving refugees and asylum seekers will be considered through this lens, and particular scrutiny can be expected, because refugees and asylum seekers may often be regarded as falling into the category of 'people in dependent or unequal relationships', one of the groups of participants to whom the

National Statement gives specific attention. The National Statement no longer uses the term 'vulnerable participants', but the concept is clearly still operative in the content of this section. Moreover, 'vulnerability' is also still very much in the minds of members of HRECs (Gillam, Guillemin, Bolitho, & Rosenthal, 2009), and is well established with the general academic discourse on research ethics. This is despite debate in the academic literature over whether the concept of 'vulnerability' is clear, meaningful and appropriate to use in relation to research ethics (Hurst, 2008).

When assessing ethics applications, HRECs have to grapple with how to assess level of risk, especially where the risk is psychological, emotional or social, rather than physical. These types of risks have an irreducibly subjective element that makes them harder to predict and quantify than physical risks. The National Statement directs HRECs to use evidence:

> In determining the existence, likelihood and severity of risks, researchers and those reviewing the research should base their assessments on the available evidence, whether qualitative or quantitative. They should consider whether to seek advice from others who have experience with the same methodology, population and research domain. (section 2.1.4, p. 18)

However, for refugee and asylum seeker research, the published evidence for the effects on participants of research participation is scare, and not easily found, since it may be embedded in studies that are primarily about something else. This puts two responsibilities on researchers in this field. The first is to be aware of and use the published evidence in their ethics applications, which will not only improve the quality of their own ethical decisions about research design, but also draw the HREC's attention to evidence that it would otherwise probably not know about. HRECs are designed to be multidisciplinary (see section 5.1.30, p. 81), but it is unlikely that a committee will have a member with specialised knowledge in this particular type of research. Given the heavy workload and time constraints under which HRECs operate, it is unlikely they will have the time and resources to pursue this evidence themselves. Researchers should supply it. The second responsibility for researchers is to be involved in the generation of evidence of the impact of participating in research on refugees and asylum seekers. Every research study, no matter what its research question or hypothesis, also presents an opportunity to gather data about research participation. This should be collected, analysed, and given a high level of importance in publication. In this way, a more substantial body of evidence can be built up, which will assist both HRECs and researchers, and ultimately will improve the experience of research participation for refugees and asylum seekers.

HRECs also have to grapple with how to evaluate the informed consent process that is put forward by the researcher. They have to assess the comprehensibility of the written information and the capacity of participants to understand not only the specific details of what they are told, but also the whole process of research and how it works, including their freedom to say 'no' if they don't want to participate. Again, evidence for making these judgements is lacking. Researchers have a responsibility to assist HRECs by providing them with any information that is relevant. In this regard, information that gives HREC members a general understanding of the particular refugee or asylum seeker group will be helpful. Some HREC members report using 'imaginative identification' as a deliberative strategy when evaluating ethics applications (Gillam et al., 2009). This involves imagining what it would be like to participate in a proposed research study, and asking oneself 'Would I be willing to do this?', or 'Would I be willing for my mother/ daughter/sister to do this?'. Their answers will be based on what they imagine an asylum seeker might think when asked by a researcher to participate in a study, and what the effect on them might be; for example, talking about how they came to leave their home country or what their hopes are for the future. Unfortunately, the capacity of HREC members (and indeed almost everyone in the community) to imaginatively identify with refugees or asylum seekers as research participants is severely limited— there is just too little commonality of experience. Researchers could usefully assist HRECs, and perhaps forestall misdirected speculation, by providing HREC members with any available evidence about the background and experiences of their proposed participant population.

Conclusion

The National Statement offers some guidance to researchers about the internal ethical aspects of refugee and asylum seeker research. In particular, it directs researchers' attention to consideration of what might be the possible risks or negative consequences to refugees or asylum seekers of participating in research, how these risks can be ameliorated, and how they weigh up against the benefits that can realistically be expected. It also directs researchers to think about how meaningful and genuinely voluntary consent can be obtained, especially for asylum seekers held in immigration detention. These considerations need to be taken into account when designing research, choosing a research population and methods of recruitment, data collection and data analysis — the substance of the ethical 'how' question. In some circumstances, these considerations should also prompt the ethical 'whether' question — whether it is ethical to conduct a particular study at all, if, for example, there will be unrealistic expectations of benefit, or persistent feelings of coercion that researchers are unlikely to be able to counter.

I have argued that researchers have an important active role to play in assisting and improving the quality of ethical review of refugee and asylum seeker research, by generating evidence that is needed for ethical evaluation, and making this available to HRECs. HRECs need evidence to draw upon in assessing risk, understanding and voluntariness. Researchers are best placed to provide this evidence. Ethical review is best practiced collaboratively, with researchers and HRECs working together to reach an understanding of what would be the most ethically appropriate way of conducting research with this particular population (see section 5.2.13, p. 84). Individual researchers can commit themselves to taking on these tasks, including the provision of relevant evidence in their ethics applications, and gathering data about the impact of research participation in every study they carry out. But there could also be an important role for an organisation or professional body of refugee and asylum seeker researchers. Such a body could be a port of call for HRECS seeking expert advice, to promote and coordinate the collection and publication of data needed for ethical review, and even to establish ethical practices and standards for the field. This would be a valuable achievement in a research field that is both crucially important and deeply contested.

References

Birman, D. (2006). Ethical issues in research with immigrants and refugees. In J.E. Trimble & C.B. Fisher (Eds.), *The handbook of ethical research with ethnocultural populations and communities* (pp. 155–177). Thousand Oaks, CA: Sage.

Düvell, F., Triandafyllidou, A., & Vollmer, B. (2010). Ethical issues in irregular migration research in Europe. *Population, Space and Place, 16*, 227–239.

Ellis, B.H., Kia-Keating, M., Yusuf, S. A., Lincoln, A., & Nur, A. (2007). Ethical research in refugee communities and the use of community participatory methods. *Transcultural Psychiatry, 44*(3), 459–481.

Gillam, L., Guillemin, M., Bolitho, A., & Rosenthal, D. (2009). Human research ethics in practice: Deliberative strategies, processes and perceptions. *Monash Bioethics Review, 28*(1), 1–17.

Hurst, S. (2008). Vulnerability in research and health care: Describing the elephant in the room? *Bioethics, 22*(4), 191–202.

Johnston, V. (2009). Australian asylum policies: Have they violated the right to health of asylum seekers? *Australian & New Zealand Journal of Public Health, 1*, 40–46.

Kirmayer, L. J., Rousseau, C., & Crepeau, F. (2004). Research ethics and the plight of refugees in detention. *Monash Bioethics Review, 23*(4), 85–92.

Mackenzie, C., McDowell, C., & Pittaway, E. (2007). Beyond 'do no harm': The challenge of constructing ethical relationships in refugee research. *Journal of Refugee Studies, 29*, 299–318.

McNeill, P. M. (2003). Public health ethics: Asylum seekers and the case for political action. *Bioethics, 17*(5–6), 487–501.

Minas, I. H. (2004). Detention and deception: Limits of ethical acceptability in detention research. *Monash Bioethics Review, 23*(4), 69–77.

National Commission for the Protection of Human Subjects of Biomedical and Behavioral Research. (1979). *The Belmont Report: Ethical principles and guidelines for the protection of human subjects of research*. Washington, DC: Office of the Secretary, Department of Health, Education, and Welfare.

National Health and Medical Research Council and Australian Vice-Chancellors Committee. (2007; updated 2009). *National statement on ethical conduct in human research*. Canberra: Australian Government.

Zion, D., Briskman, L., & Loff, B. (2010). Returning to history: The ethics of researching asylum seeker health in Australia. *American Journal of Bioethics, 10*(2), 48–56.

3

To Respect or Protect? Whose Values Shape the Ethics of Refugee Research?

Sandy Gifford

In early 2000, a colleague and I submitted an application to our university HREC for a pilot project to modify a series of standardised wellbeing instruments for a longitudinal study of refugee[1] youth settlement. The pilot study was collaborative in that we worked with a small group of young adults with refugee backgrounds to design sampling and data collection strategies and a set of research tools or instruments that could be used to gather qualitative and quantitative information about settlement experiences (Gifford, Bakopanos, Kaplan, & Correa-Velez, 2007; Gifford, Correa-Velez, & Sampson, 2009). Although the ethics application was straightforward, it was returned by the HREC as not approved. We were not surprised when our application was returned because in our experience, human ethics applications with/on refugees almost never get approved outright. However, we were surprised about the *reason* it had been returned. The HREC took objection to one of the questions we were using to explore how scaled items could be best presented

— a question chosen by the group of young adults collaborating with us on the pilot: *'How much do you like ice cream?'* and *'Given a choice between ice cream and pizza, which would you choose first?'*. The HREC judged these questions as having the potential to cause harm to resettled refugee youth because they were refugees. The logic was that being refugees, these youth would have experienced starvation and like other forms of trauma, questions about food were seen as a risk to re-traumatise. We were asked to attend the next meeting of the HREC to explain our choice of foods such as 'ice cream and pizza' for this population and why we believed that these questions were unlikely to cause harm — to re-traumatise this group.

My colleague attended the meeting where, in less than five minutes and with virtually no discussion, the project was approved. My colleague explained that the committee was surprised to see that she — the researcher — 'looked' very much like some of the young people in the study who like her, had been born in Africa. She described to the committee that although all of the youth had a refugee past, they also were like other teenagers who enjoyed sweets and 'junk' food. She went on to point out that not all refugees were from Africa, not all refugees had been poor or starving and not all were still held victims by their past. The committee approved the study.

The second story relates to a media arts research project with young people from refugee backgrounds. The project was a partnership among researchers (led by myself and a colleague), government, youth service organisations and arts media organisations. The project aimed to investigate whether a cultural development approach through digital arts media could help these youth maintain their social connections with friends and family still overseas and if this in turn could support successful settlement in Australia. The research was designed to be ethnographic with researchers using participatory observation of project activities. A multilayered process of informed consent was developed and we took care to ensure that all participants understood and had given their consent (both verbal and written) to the research. One of the workshops was conducted by a group of community artists who were teaching media art skills to the participants. The workshop began with introductions that were mostly for the benefit of the artists since the participants and the researchers all knew each other well by this stage in the project. However, when the researchers introduced themselves, the group of community artists expressed their view that it was unethical to do research with these refugee youth in the context of an arts-based project. Especially in relation to refugee participants, research was viewed to be incompatible with the goals of youth development through art media. Indeed, two of the artists clearly expressed their dismay and argued that research in general was intrusive and harmful for refugee youth.

Both of these case studies highlight the ways in which particular *values* shape the kinds of judgements that are made about the ethics of research that focuses on people with refugee backgrounds. In both cases, the category of refugee is naturalised in that as a cultural concept it comes to take on a particular set of implicit shared meanings. The positions of both the HREC and the community artists about the meaning of the cultural category 'refugee' highlight how values and identities shape the ways we think about 'what is right' in the ethics of research with people with refugee backgrounds. The first story illustrates the power of the 'refugee' label and the implicit assumptions that it confers. The fact that my colleague 'looked African' but was not and had never been a refugee, confronted a range of stereotypes held by members of the HREC about African-born people and people with refugee backgrounds, and led them to re-assess notions of autonomy and vulnerability within this context. In the second case, community artists brought their own values to play that articulated both their own group identity and how they saw the identities of the participants. The artists saw themselves engaged in participatory, emancipatory practices that valued difference, marginality and promoted youth development. In contrast, research was seen to be a mechanism of control, of surveillance and counter to the liberating space of art making. In both case studies, the voices and values of the participants themselves — to be something other than a refugee — became lost in the tussle between the *value cultures* of HREC members, artists and researchers.

In this chapter, I first begin by discussing what I mean by value cultures and how an anthropological lens might open up different ways to understand how and why different parties who share the same concerns to promote respect and autonomy for refugees, often clash when it comes to what is ethical research in this field. Second, I explore the value cultures and tensions that arise over differences of opinion between HRECs, service providers and community organisations, and researchers and ask whether values are or ought to be, relative or absolute. Finally, I consider the power of the refugee label and ask in whose interest does the process of ethical review and surveillance operate? Importantly, to what extent do HRECs unintentionally reinforce refugee victimhood by prioritising values of protecting over respecting?

Ethics, Value Cultures and Fields of Difference in Refugee Research

There is wide agreement that the ethics of research with people who are or have been refugees is complex, changing and challenging (Ellis, Kia-Keating, Yusuk, Lincoln, & Nur, 2007; Siber, 2009). There is a growing literature addressing these challenges and common themes focus on the various aspects of risk to vulnerable participants, the active involvement of refugees in research and on issues surrounding participant agency in the research (Hugman, Bartolomei, & Pittaway, 2011; Hugman, Pittaway, & Bartolomei, 2011; Mackenzie, McDowell, & Pittaway, 2007). Another important area of scholarship concerns the inadequacies of institutional ethic committees where principles often designed for medical research are applied to the complexities of research with refugees and other vulnerable or marginalised groups (Perry, 2011). At stake are interpretations of 'vulnerability', the meanings of which are highly dependent on context and which, when not taken into account, can fail to recognise the agency of refugees as research participants (Perry, 2011). Indeed, Kirmayer and Rousseau (2004) have highlighted the moral imperative to conduct research that goes against the prevailing ideologies of HRECs, as in the case of research into refugees in detention. Here, in relation to detainees in Australia, research may be only possible without official permission or with deception. Indeed, HRECs run the risk of colluding with new forms of state power by preventing the documentation of forms of abuse precisely because of the illegality of doing research in these institutional spaces (Kirmayer & Rousseau, 2004). Importantly, Kirmayer and Rousseau argue that research that cannot be undertaken via formal channels as for example, documenting the plight of detainees, is a form of legitimate illegal action. Such are the complexities of navigating the ethical landscape of research with refugees and other forced migrants.

In addressing these complexities, the Refugee Studies Centre, University of Oxford (2007) has developed a set of ethical guidelines that focus on 'good practice' — being informative and descriptive rather than authoritarian or prescriptive (p. 172). The guidelines explicitly recognise that the field of forced migration research is complex, and that an ethics of research cannot be guided by any single set of moral precepts, nor can they take the form of rigid instructions set by institutional bodies (p. 171). Further, they address not only refugees as the subjects of research, but also the wider field of stakeholders including sponsors, gatekeepers, governments and broader society. While not ignoring the need to protect research subjects, they recognise that in reality, this may not always be possible. Instead, emphasis is given to the importance of relationships between the participants and researchers being based on trust, negotiation, the rights of participants and the respective roles, rights and obligations of parties other than research participants. Importantly, the guidelines aim to provide a *practical* framework for researchers in anticipating potential challenges in a complex and rapidly changing field and to assist them in making informed decisions in this context.

It is within this complex context that I return to the focus of this chapter — the clash of values in regard to what is ethical in refugee research. I begin with the premise that what is at stake are the different value cultures held by the various actors in the refugee research field and the tensions that arise when these clash. In first considering culture, I draw on the ideas of Arjun Appadurai (1996), who conceptualises culture not so much as a thing but rather as process: '... the process of naturalizing a subset of differences that have been mobilized to articulate group identity' (p. 15). Importantly, culture as process forms itself around identity and difference in relation to something else. It is then, both situated and relational. Put another way, culture is about the making of collective identities that are different to an *other* — and these differences in turn reinforce the shared identities of a group, which again reinforce the differences of those who are outsiders. Appadurai suggests that it is the markers of group difference that highlight contestations of values about difference (p. 14).

This leads us to consider the concept of *value*. From an anthropological perspective, Graeber (2001) suggests that we can think of values as 'conceptions of the desirable' (Kluckhohn as cited in Graeber, 2001) or as '... ideas about what people *ought* to want' (Graeber 2001, p. 3). Values are shared ideas about what people consider to be good, proper, meaningful and importantly, as Graeber argues, how these meanings turn into desire (p. ix). Again, from an anthropological perspective, values are not absolute, and some of the early ethnographic work compared the cultures of people living in the same physical environment but who had vastly different value systems. For the purposes of this chapter, values are the collective, shared ideas about what is right (or ought to be right), they are often implicit, shape group identity and they guide what is meaningful and correct social engagement in the world. Group differences commonly focus on the contestation of values and it is to this I now turn.

I use the concept *value cultures* to bring together the idea of culture as collective identity constructed in relation to an other — in this regard, constructed in relation to ideas of what is right and desirable in the world. Bringing to the fore different *value cultures* as they apply to the ethics of refugee research can help to shed light on how, what would appear to be the sharing of common interests can turn into a battlefield of contested difference and ill intentions. There are at least three value cultures that we can draw out of these two case studies above, value cultures that articulate themselves by way of identity and difference with respect to the right way to protect and do no harm to refugee subjects. These are firstly, the value culture of the HREC, secondly the value culture of the community artists, and thirdly, the value culture of the researchers. Conflicts between these value cultures become apparent when issues of identity and difference are at stake. I argue that many of the tensions and conflicts that arise in refugee research between researchers, ethics committees, service providers, gatekeepers and stakeholders can be understood as clashes between taken for granted values — values that shape group identities. In particular contexts where multiple groups have vested interests, these value cultures come into conflict and highlight the sharp divides between group identities where the imperative to 'protect' and to 'do no harm' have vastly different meanings. Further, I argue that the naturalising of 'refugee' often results in erasing refugee voices from the ethics nexus.

The process of reviewing a research study involving people who are, might be or have been, refugees is informed by a set of core values that implicitly shape how we understand what it is to be human and then, what it is to be a refugee. Hayden (2006), in considering what kinds of persons we understand refugees to be, argues that 'the person ... is a cultural category that refers to how we conceptualise the nature of the self' (p. 481) and that within the international refugee regime, a refugee is constructed in relation to a 'western' person — an individual who is autonomous, has free will and the same human rights as others — all humans being held to be equal. The refugee individual is constructed as a person lacking these qualities or characteristics: 'To the degree that refugees are represented as lacking autonomy, they are deprived of a funda-mental aspect of what we consider our humanity' (Hayden, 2006, p. 481). Importantly, Hayden argues that the way we conceptualise the refugee is shaped by both western assump-tions about their needs and interests and by the interests of the organisations and people working with them. Thus, the refugee is constructed as a person without — a person in lack.

It is a fallacy to assume that the refugee in exile, while often lacking in autonomy, is also lacking in agency (Harrell-Bond & Voutira, 2007; Kibreab, 2004). Within the international refugee regime, humanitarian organisations often reinforce depend-ency in the form of aid as charity and obligations that stem from humanitarian aid (Fassin, 2012; Harrell-Bond, 2002). Malkki (1996) argues that one of the consequences of the humanitarian refugee regime is what she refers to as a process of dehistoricisation — which is the erasure of individual his-tories where personal identities are reduced to a collective identity woven around notions of persecution, vulnerability, dependency and need. The question arises, what kind of a person is the refugee resettled? I argue that the process of dehistoricisation continues to define the identity of these indi-viduals. It is difficult for the migrant who has arrived in Australia on a humanitarian visa to shed the refugee label and it is equally difficult for the host society, its institutions and practices to relate to such persons in ways other than as refugees. The fact that this powerful labelling process is being increasingly resisted by migrants with refugee backgrounds themselves (Aidani, 2010; Kumsa, 2006) has had little impact on prevailing practice more generally, and this is especially the case in relation to the values which inform the ethics of research with resettled refugees.

Value Cultures of Institutional Human Ethics Committees

The National Health and Medical Research Council (NHMRC, 2007; updated 2009), *National Statement on Ethical Conduct in Human Research* (the National Statement) begins with a discussion of the values that guide the relationships between researchers and research participants. It states that '... respect for human beings, research merit and integrity, justice, and beneficence — help to shape that relationship as one of trust, mutual responsibility and ethical equality' (p. 11). The value of respect is highlighted as being central:

> Among these values, respect is central. It involves recognising that each human being has value in himself or herself, and that this value must inform all interaction between people. Such respect includes recognising the value of human autonomy — the capacity to determine one's own life and make one's own decisions. But respect goes further than this. It also involves providing for the protection of those with diminished or no autonomy, as well as empowering them where possible and protecting and helping people wherever it would be wrong not to do so. (section 1, p. 11)

This preamble clearly sets the framework for HRECs in their consideration of the conduct of research with persons with refugee backgrounds. However, it has been my experience both as a researcher submitting applications for review and as a member of two HRECs (one a hospital and one a university committee) that in reviewing applications, the existence of any subjects who are or have been refugees results in a focus on their refugeeness to the exclusion of any other criteria of personhood. The refugee label — whether in exile or in resettlement — comes to shift the focus of the value of respect from that of an autonomous person capable of determining their own life and making their own decisions to that of a person with diminished or no autonomy. The role of the HREC thus becomes focused solely on the need to protect — but from what is often not clear. Assumed vulnerability attributed to refugeeness has the effect of erasing the possibility for potential participants to exercise their own autonomy and make their own decisions about their engagement with social research.

The HREC that judged questions about ice cream and pizza to be potentially traumatising failed to acknowledge a range of other identities among these youth — that they were teenagers with similar likes and dislikes to other young people their age, that they represented a range of ethnic, cultural and socioeconomic backgrounds, that they lived in a range of family situations with a diversity of values about gender roles and family responsibilities. The young people in our study all considered these factors more important than that they had been refugees. Indeed, the assumption by the HREC that these youth needed to be protected because of their refugeeness could be cast as a lack of respect for the ability of these young people to make their own decisions and for their capacity to determine their lives. By uncritically prioritising the refugee identity, HRECs run the risk of further disempowering research participants with refugee backgrounds and erasing their voices from the social research arena.

A second consequence of the imperative to protect is the insistence by some HRECs on the provision of trauma counseling services regardless of the nature of the research and its potential risks. This 'therapeutising' of refugeeness (Marlowe, 2010) runs the risk of reinforcing dependency among people with refugee backgrounds and at the same time, serves the interests of a broader array of institutions in regards to what they consider feasible or desirable in their management of refugees (Hayden, 2006). In sum, the risk of an ethnocentric focus on the part of HRECs when it comes to refugee research is that it can lead to a blindness to other social criteria and contexts that may be more important than refugeeness. The challenge for HRECs is to explicitly interrogate when being or having been a refugee makes a difference to a proposed piece of social research and why. This requires a standing back from the implicit values that HRECs might bring to what it is they consider a refugee to be. An essentialising of refugeeness leads to prioritising values to protect above values to respect indicating that the value cultures of HRECs tend to favour the former over the latter. This in turn effectively erases any possibility of conceptualising the research subject in terms other that one with a particular set of refugee vulnerabilities and precludes consideration of factors that might be more important to the particular research.

Value Cultures of Service Providers and Community Organisations

Community organisations and service providers working in the refugee sector are often motivated by a range of humanitarian values — to aid, to protect, to build capacity, to advocate for or on behalf of, to address needs — to do good in the world. Doing good can become as much an identity for individuals as for institutions. Particularly in the nongovernment, and community sector, values and identity play a strong role in shaping the motivations of its workers — where monetary remuneration is low and larger institutional structures mitigate against positive, more radical short and long-term social change. Service providers and community organisations are often fierce gatekeepers when it comes to refugee research. As gatekeepers, they may see themselves as refugee protectors — from outsiders and from institutional practices and forms of power that would do them harm. The potential for conflict with the academic research sector is high especially when it comes to refugee research. As with HRECs, those working in the community sector are often guilty of unintentionally essentialising the construct of 'refugee' and in doing so, see their mission as protecting and advocating on behalf of these persons who are deemed to be vulnerable because of their assumed identity. In this regard, as with HRECs, the mandate to protect erases the courtesy to respect. And this in turn removes any possibilities of agency among individuals and communities who once were refugees and who are now their clients.

The second case study of the community artist's reaction to the ethics of research with young people with refugee backgrounds can be interpreted as the research being seen as a threat to their own set of cultural practices and identities, which are made and remade in contrast to the assumed identities of refugee youth. The practices of youth development through art can only be executed with vulnerable, marginalised bodies, and it is this vulnerability made visible (or possible) through their refugeeness that in turn legitimates the culture and identities of community artists. Liberating agency through art can only be performed on a vulnerable subject and refugee youth are the blank canvasses for this artistic expression. The researchers as participatory observers, in this context, are outsiders and moreover, outsiders with a different set of values in relation to their research subjects — which include both the artists and the participants. The researchers in this case study, one of whom also had a refugee background, saw the research participants as young people first; newly arrived migrants to Australia second and third, also with refugee experiences. Importantly, the researchers explicitly worked against an essentialising of these youth, an approach informed as much by their own experiences as by the broader theoretical literature that informed their own positions in the research field. Once again, the imperative to protect rather than to respect stems from a particular value culture shaping identity and practice among community artists working within a youth development framework. This value culture stands in contrast to that of the researchers and resulted, in this case, in a clash of cultural values in relation to the construct of 'refugee' youth. Importantly and somewhat ironically, possibilities for transformation for this group of youth through art were limited by the very values about ethics of research held by the group of community artists 'doing good'.

Value Cultures of Researchers

The value cultures of researchers in relation to what is ethical in refugee research are a complex and contested site. On the one hand, there are those who argue that the rigour and objectivity of the research methodology must come before anything else because it is the quality of the results that counts in the translation of knowledge or 'evidence' to policy and practice. On the other hand, there are those who argue that the other imperatives — the realities of refugees — take precedence over strict adherence to principles of objective scientific inquiry. Researcher value cultures are further complicated by the ongoing methodological debates between qualitative and quantitative approaches to social inquiry and by disciplinary traditions to research. Refugee research is widely regarded as being inherently multidisciplinary and this is a key strength. However in practice, the tensions between method, discipline and role of the researcher in relation to the research subject — remain problematic.

These tensions are played out in ongoing debates about the ethics of refugee research. For example, a key site of tension is research regarding asylum seekers where access to information and people is prohibited. Kirmayer and Rousseau (2004) argue for the legitimacy of what they refer to as 'legitimate illegal action' when researchers use deception to gain access to interview people held in detention. Correa-Velez and Gifford (2007) argue that asylum seekers have a right to be counted and that it is unethical for governments to withhold data about asylum seekers and people held in detention, from researchers. Harrell-Bond (2002) asks the hard questions about whether refugee research can ever be humanitarian and Harrell-Bond and Voutira (2007) have long argued for the centrality of the 'refugee voice' in research. Finally, questions about the role of the researcher as advocate remain hotly debated with those against arguing that this undermines the rigor of the research — and its objectivity.

These debates have given rise to a culture of critical reflection among many researchers in this field — regardless of whether or not they wish to engage in these critiques: 'What are the pros and cons of the researcher being an insider or outsider?', 'Qualitative or quantitative approaches?', 'Participatory or researcher driven?', 'Who can speak for whom?', 'What does one do with 'risky' data?'. Although these issues are being productively interrogated in the published literature (Hugman, Bartolomei, et al., 2011; Hugman, Pittaway, et al., 2011) the research path leading into and out of refugee research remains perilous. The value cultures of researchers that inform the ethics of refugee research are multiple and contentious and are likely to remain so into the future. However, this tension is a key strength precisely because a researcher, whether they are a student, an evaluator, an academic, an insider or outsider cannot enter the field without having their taken-for-granted values challenged and reflected back to them in some form along the way. In sum, the value cultures of researchers are often more exposed and thus more open to 'attack' than those of HRECs and service providers and community organisations.

Value Cultures of People With Refugee Experiences

What of the value cultures of people who are or have been refugees, asylum seekers, forced migrants? This field of inquiry has barely been explored, which testifies to a general invisibility of 'subject' voices in refugee research more broadly (Harrell-Bond & Voutira 2007). Research from the 'inside' in remains problematic largely for its absence. Aidani (this volume), and Kumsa (2006) are examples of the exceptions to the above in that they make clear their own position as researcher/former refugee and from this position, make important critiques of the values that are brought to refugee research. Importantly, they challenge the essentialised and naturalised refugee — the label 'once a refugee always a refugee' that sticks to people with refugee backgrounds or experiences. This critique is important because it challenges the implicit values that HRECs, service providers, community organisations and researchers alike all too often bring to the field of 'refugee' research. Malkki (1996) argues that people who are or were refugees are represented as dehistoricised subjects — or in other words, their personal, social and political histories and subjectivities are erased leaving them only with identities of victimhood. Importantly, any possibility of agency is rendered invisible and this I argue, lies at the heart of the problem of whose values inform refugee research. In a context where the research subjects are represented as victims, it is far easier to shape a research ethics as one that protects over one that respects.

Discussion: Whose Values? In Whose Interest?

The above discussion leads to the key questions of this chapter. Whose values shape the ethics of refugee research? Why is this terrain so often one of conflict and contestation? Where is the agency of the research subject — the community or individual with refugee experience — in all of this? I want to conclude with a third story — that of one of my doctoral students, Anne, whose study aimed to explore the experiences of being a mother in a new country within the context of refugee settlement. The project involved conducting in-depth interviews with recently arrived women with children. Anne spent much time agonising about how she would enter the field, how she would represent herself, how she would be sure not to re-traumatise the women, how she would ensure informed consent, was her research important enough to these women, how could she repay them for their time, and a dozen other concerns. Finally she had to just jump in. One of first interviews she lined up was with a woman, Ruth, who was a single mother, had six children, had spent years living in a refugee camp during which time she had organised food and education programs for orphans — and there were many of these children in the camp. As Anne began to explain the research and the informed consent to her research participant, Ruth abruptly reversed the roles and began to interview Anne. The interview lasted more than an hour during which Ruth set the research agenda, clearly articulated what she would and would not talk about and invited Anne (rather directly) to begin by sharing her own background and personal experiences about being a woman — challenging her about her status as a single woman without children — in Australia. As the supervisor, what I observed was a subtle but significant shift in values held by Anne from those focused on protecting to those of respecting. Importantly, this shifted Anne's approach to the research, to the women who were now more interlocutors than participants or subjects and opened up possibilities for research that was something more than a focus on how refugee mothers cope in a settlement context.

In addressing the central question of this chapter — many different values, in what I have described as value cultures, shape the ethics of refugee research. These value cultures are implicit and normative and are the substance around which group identities are formed. Importantly, these value cultures express shared ideas — often taken for granted — about what is *right*. The conflicts that often arise between different groups around what is ethical in relation to refugee research stem from threats to the implicit value cultures of each. These threats translate to fundamental attacks on group identities and the worthiness of particular missions or projects. But what is really at stake in this clash of value cultures is the *refugee* — produced as a naturalised, essentialised subject — and who serves as a mirror reflecting back the values that shape the projects of the various stakeholders.

There are no easy answers to these dilemmas — especially in a field where all the players are well intentioned. The values that drive the ethics of research with refugees are neither relative nor absolute. Refugee research is always situational and contingent. The intent 'to do the right thing' when it comes to the ethics of refugee research, is often a reflection of particular value cultures of specific organisations and groups — the stakeholders if you will — in the refugee field. The conflicts that arise between different stakeholders, for example, among HRECs, community organisations, and researchers, are often about contesting particular identities invested in and expressed through their respective value cultures.

What is at stake in this contest of values? At the core are the personal and professional identities of the individuals involved in judgements about what is ethical when it comes to refugee research. These interests, although well intended, can act to override or erase those of the individuals and communities who are or have been refugees. The question that should be asked in this situation is what is the refugee? There is a need for recognition that the refugee layer is only one layer — albeit an important one — in the life stories of individuals and communities. And if we put this recognition first, then a common ground based first on respect might be a starting point for negotiating a stable common base that informs a fluid field when it comes to values that inform refugee research.

Endnote

1. The term *refugee* is problematic from many perspectives. First, the term is used not only to identify people who are found to be refugees under the formal UNHCR definition, but it is used to refer to a wide array of people who are forced and/or undocumented migrants. Second, the term is often used indiscriminately to identify people who have been, but are no longer refugees. This chapter focused on research with people who have been, but are no longer, refugees. The language to describe such persons is clumsy — people with refugee backgrounds, humanitarian settlers, people who have arrived on humanitarian visas, and so on. In this chapter, I used both the terms *refugee* and *people with refugee backgrounds* depending on context, while recognising them in places, my use of the term remains problematic.

References

Aidani, M. (2010). Existential accounts of Iranian displacement and the cultural meanings of categories. *Journal of Intercultural Studies, 31*, 121–143.

Aidani, M. (2013). Face to face: Ethics and responsibility. In K. Block, E. Riggs & N. Haslam (Eds.), *Values and vulnerabilities: The ethics of research with refugees and asylum seekers.* Brisbane, Australia: Australian Academic Press.

Appadurai, A. (1996). *Modernity at large: Cultural dimensions of globalization.* Minneapolis: University of Minnesota Press.

Correa-Velez, I., & Gifford, S.M. (2007). When the right to be counted doesn't count: The politics and challenges of researching the health of asylum seekers. *Critical Public Health, 17*, 273–281.

Ellis, H., Kia-Keating, B.M., Yusuf, S.A., Lincoln, A, & Nur, A. (2007). Ethical research in refugee communities and the use of community participatory methods. *Transcultural Psychiatry, 44*, 459–481.

Fassin, D. (2012). *Humanitarian reason: A moral history of the present.* Berkeley & Los Angeles: University of California Press.

Gifford, S. M., Bakopanos, C., Kaplan, I., & Correa-Velez, I. (2007). Meaning or measurement? Researching the social contexts of health and settlement among newly-arrived refugee youth in Melbourne, Australia. *Journal of Refugee Studies, 20*, 414–440.

Gifford, S. M., Correa-Velez, I., & Sampson, R. (2009). *Good starts for recently arrived youth with refugee backgrounds: Promoting wellbeing in the first three years of settlement in Melbourne, Australia.* La Trobe Refugee Research Centre, La Trobe University.

Graeber, D. (2001). *Toward an anthropological theory of value: The false coin of our own dreams.* New York, NY: Palgrave.

Harrell-Bond, B. (2002). Can humanitarian work with refugees be humane? *Human Rights Quarterly, 24*, 51–85.

Harrell-Bond, B., & Voutira, E. (2007). In search of 'invisible' actors: Barriers to access in refugee research. *Journal of Refugee Studies, 20*, 281–298.

Hayden, B. (2006). What's in a name? The nature of the individual in refugee studies. *Journal of Refugee Studies, 19*, 471–487.

Hugman, R., Bartolomei, L., & Pittaway, E. (2011). Human agency and the meaning of 'informed consent': Reflections on research with refugees. *Journal of Refugee Studies, 24*, 656–671.

Hugman, R., Pittaway, E., & Bartolomei, L. (2011). When 'do no harm' is not enough: The ethics of research with refugees and other vulnerable groups. *British Journal of Social Work, 41*, 1271–1287.

Kibreab, G. (2004). Pulling the wool over the eyes of the strangers: Refugee deceit and trickery in institutionalized settings. *Journal of Refugee Studies, 17*, 2–26.

Kirmayer, L.J., & Rousseau, C. (2004). Research ethics and the plight of refugees in detention. *Monash Bioethics Review, 23*, 85–92.

Kumsa, M.K. (2006). 'No! I'm not a refugee!' The poetics of be-longing among young Oromos in Toronto. *Journal of Refugee Studies, 19*, 231–255.

Mackenzie, C., McDowell, C., & Pittaway, E. (2007). Beyond 'Do no harm': The challenge of constructing ethical relationships in refugee research. *Journal of Refugee Studies, 20*, 299–319.

Malkki, L.H. (1996). Speechless emissaries: Refugees, humanitarianism, and dehistoricization. *Cultural Anthropology, 11*, 377-404.

Marlowe, J.M. (2010). Beyond the discourse of trauma: Shifting the focus on Sudanese refugees. *Journal of Refugee Studies, 23*, 183–198.

National Health and Medical Research Council (2007; updated 2009). *National statement on ethical conduct in human research.* Canberra: Australian Government.

Perry, K. H. (2011). Ethics, vulnerability, and speakers of other languages: How university IRBs (do not) speak to research involving refugee participants. *Qualitative Inquiry, 17,* 899-912.

Refugee Studies Centre. (2007). Ethical guidelines for good research practice. *Refugee Survey Quarterly, 26,* 163–172.

Siber, J. (2009). Refugee research: Strangers in a strange land. *Journal of Empirical Research on Human Research Ethics, 4,* 35–36.

PART

2

METHODOLOGICAL APPROACHES TO ETHICAL RESEARCH

CHAPTER

4

Researching Displacement(s)

Christopher McDowell

The author's experience[1] of sitting on various university non-medical ethics committees representing social science and politics departments suggests that third only behind research on children and some psychological experimentation entailing deliberate deception, research on displaced populations guarantees the most lively discussion and furrowed brows. Where research involves young refugees, acts of illegality or the recalling of traumatic episodes, the call for additional information, safeguards and conditions on research, can be expected to mount as discussion is prolonged. Increasingly, the ethics approval process, made concrete in ever lengthening clearance application forms, will seek additional information on recruitment, consent, confidentiality and risk and harm where research subjects include so called vulnerable groups; and migrants and refugees are now typically added alongside minors, patients and prisoners as potentially vulnerable research subjects. The explicit assumption being that migrants and refugees constitute a social group who by virtue of their particular circumstances and situation may lack the means to adequately protect themselves against coercion or harm in the research process. This chapter considers why it has become the norm in ethics review procedures to construct 'displaced' people as a category of vulnerability and what this construction, and the protection such categorisations have led to, may tell us about understandings of autonomy, agency and responsibility at a time in history where displacement has come to embody risks and dangers on the hard edge of globalisation. The author tends to concur with Furedi's (2011) recent criticism of institutional cultures that are unquestioningly inclined to treat the individual as 'vulnerable' thus underestimating the fact that people, even in stressful situations, are more robust than we give them credit for, and capable of making moral decisions.

It is argued that this reidentification of displaced people is in part a product of global policy making, reinterpretations of international law, and operational practice responding to complex population movements in areas of crisis. The chapter investigates the assumptions that underpin the association of displacement with vulnerability. It considers the nature of that vulnerability and the implications for ethical research. It shows how a particular kind of 'refugeeness' has been projected onto other types of displacement and in so doing has set the template for an understanding of the displacement condition more generally and academics' ethical responsibilities directly. The author is sceptical about the merit of such generalised assumptions about vulnerability, autonomy and agency in situations of displacement and would rather urge researchers and ethics committees alike to disaggregate displacement experiences within and between the main causes of displacement — conflict, natural disasters, environmental change, and development — and regard for the purposes of ethical review, each displacement situation and individual circumstances as unique.

The chapter further notes that based on regular contact with academics engaged in displacement-related research, while there is concern about what Shore (2008) has described as the creeping 'audit culture' in universities (evidence of which some see in ethics review processes), there is general support for the idea that migrants and refugees as subjects of research demand special consideration and supervisors are sensitising their research students to the ethical issues involved. Part of the reason for this acceptance may be because, as Black (2001) has noted, a disproportionate amount of refugee research has been of an applied nature, conducted at the request of states and international organisations, funded by governments and focused on immediate and rather narrow policy issues rather than following an independent research agenda. Social scientists have long been uncomfortable with applied policy directed research (Caplan, 2003; James, 2007) and the politicisation of their work it entails; for refugee researchers there is added discomfort about the direction of humanitarian and political interventions in displacement situations and their outcomes. That concern centres on the ways in which the standard range of interventions — building camps as a first resort (Harrell-Bond, 1986), gearing up a humanitarian machine that is increasingly politicised, privatised and militarised (Duffield, 2007), restricting alternative routes to protection such as asylum, and expediting return and repatriation (McDowell, 2006; McDowell & Eastmond, 2002) — by and large serve the interests of states and work towards restoring a diplomatically agreed order that is strikingly similar to the order that existed before the conflict broke out. For academics, elevating the displaced as a category of concern in the academic ethics review process may serve to alleviate some of the frustrations of conducting research in this politicised arena by forthrightly acknowledging the moral and conscious agency of those being researched; and in so doing bring to the surface some of the underlying structures of domination that give shape to refugee and migration policy, and to the experience of being a refugee.

Refugeeness and Disaggregating Displacement

This volume was published at a historic moment in global refugee policy. The East African drought of 2010 and 2011, and the prolonged civil conflict in Somalia, provided the context for a significant reinterpretation of refugee law and practice. The UNHCR, under its head Antonio Guterres, completed the task he began in 2005 by finally repositioning his organisation as the agency for the globally displaced rather than only being an organisation that, according to its mandate set down in the 1951 Refugee Convention, looks after the interests of international refugees (i.e., people who have fled violence or persecution, have crossed an international border, and who can no longer avail themselves of the protection of the state in which they are a citizen). Guterres was responding to a mass of academic litera-ture, humanitarian evaluations, and past failings of the United Nations (UN; in Srebrenica, Rwanda, and the Great Lakes Region in general), which together provided evidence that the current international system, based on the 1951 Convention and a web of intergovernmental and nongovernmental humanitar-ian organisations with sector specific responsibilities, was insuf-ficient to protect the whole range of displaced people caught up in conflicts, disasters and oppressive acts of states. Over a 6-year period he stretched the mandate of the UNHCR and expanded the definition of 'people of concern' beyond cross-border refugees to include internally displaced persons (IDPs; people displaced by conflict within the borders of their countries), migrants caught up in emergency situations[2], and those dis-placed by environmental crises to include climate change impacts. In August, 2011, the newly enlarged Dadaab Refugee Camp in Kenya began filling up with environmental displacees living among conflict refugees accessing the same international protection and humanitarian assistance under the auspices of the UNHCR.

As a consequence of the decisions taken by the UN, the concept of the refugee as a person who is vulnerable and enti-tled to international protection was extended to millions of additional people for whom migration is the best option to cope with hardships and risk: those people were defined as being in a 'refugee like situation' and therefore 'of concern' to the UNHCR. A parallel legal process was underway which at the same time sought to broaden the legal definition of a refugee to include those displaced by events and processes other than conflict as defined in international humanitarian law (McDowell & Morrell, 2010) and to hold states accountable for any human rights violations that occur in situations of displacement. Pre-eminent among these measures was the attempt by the UN to promote the recognition and uptake by states of the UN Guiding Principles on Internal Displacement, and in Addis Ababa an endorsement by African governments of the African Union (AU) Convention for the Protection and Assistance of Internally Displaced Persons in Africa, both of which held states responsible for addressing the conditions that create displace-ment, avoiding displacement and protecting those displaced. The AU Convention went further than the Guiding Principles including in its definition of displacement causation, develop-ment and poverty. The emerging doctrine of the Responsibility to Protect (R2P), which had its roots in Francis Deng's idea of 'sov-ereignty as responsibility' (Deng, 1996) (itself a founding princi-ple of the UN Guiding Principles), held out the prospect that states who fail to honour their responsibility to protect displaced citizens could find themselves subject to international action at the UN including military-led humanitarian intervention.

Taken together, these normative developments signal an important reconceptualising of refugees and displacement, erasing the former boundaries, established in the aftermath of World War II, that separated categories of displacement by geo-graphical location (crossing or not crossing a border) and cau-sation (individual persecution). This occurred, as has been explained, because the post-1951 system for dealing with the globally displaced produced a protective umbrella with so many holes that most vulnerable people were excluded from rather than included in the systems of international protection, and where protection was provided it frequently fell well short of what was expected and hoped for. It further arose because of academic and operational evidence that contemporary forced migration flows were far more complex than in the past, they rarely conform to neat definitional boundaries, but are rather 'mixed' with conflict refugees in flight alongside those fleeing deteriorating environmental conditions and others seeking work in another country (the so called 'asylum-migration nexus'). Attempts at disentangling these flows (see for example the so called Pacific and Mediterranean Solutions) have proven politically fraught (Kneebone, 2007). Research on displacement, and decisions around the ethics of doing research among displaced people, is taking place in a context where the particular situation of refugees, more specifically, *refugees in camps,* is providing the paradigm for the whole range of forced migration situations.

The elements of this refugee camp 'refugeeness' include the characterisation of the refugee as someone who is buffeted by external events, who lacks choices and opportunities to change the course of their life, and who comes to depend on international charity and assistance. Essentially, the refugee is regarded as someone who lacks power, autonomy and dignity, and occupies a liminal political space (the refugee camp). Refugee women in camps exemplify the most extreme form of vulnerability with numerous studies revealing how women and children experience sexual violence in camps that lack physical security (absence of guards, poor lighting, cramped conditions) and create the conditions that place women in danger (women and children being forced to collect firewood from beyond the camps fences, being dependent on men in the camps for rations or access to medicine). Decisions to either prolong the existence of a camp in a particular location, to determine its size and type of intake, to decommission and close the camp or return the refugees to their country of origin are taken by governments and UN agencies in Geneva and New York on the basis of political demands (most frequently to work within a timeframe itself determined by the holding of internationally sponsored elections designed to normalise a post-conflict state; see Mcdowell & Eastmond, 2002) and the availability of financing. Refugees have no voice in these decisions. There are very few detailed ethnographies of refugees camps, and as James (2007) has noted, most studies are commissioned and involve working very closely with government and international organisations who act quite literally as gatekeepers determining the space within which research is conducted, and most research is fragmentary, brief and hardly ever after the sun has gone down (Vogler, 2006). While camp literature provides substantial evidence of dependency and lack of autonomy on the part of the refugee (Harrell-Bond, 1996), there are also important studies that discuss a degree of cultural vitality in camps (James, 2007) of radical and engaged politics, and of resistance to authority. These are however, exceptions that do not alter the prevailing understanding of encamped 'refugeeness'.

Asylum Seekers

How accurate though is this prevailing understanding of 'refugeeness' for displacement and displaced people in noncamp situations? Forced displacement in internal conflict and in wars between states creates not only encamped refugee populations, but also what are commonly termed conflict migrants. Within countries, they are officially termed IDPs and internationally, asylum seekers, that is people who cross borders and who aim to make applications for refugee recognition mainly in a western country. For this latter group, studies have shown (McDowell, 1996; Linley, 2010) that asylum seeking involves a whole range of migration strategies which require high degrees of organisation and the mobilisation of economic, human and social capital to flee danger, cross borders frequently illegally, arrange paperwork, pay agents and smugglers, and evade authorities in order to join fellow countrymen en route and in the country of asylum. It requires additional significant resources to make an application for refugee status and to find employment while the process unfolds. On arrival and in settlement, asylum seekers, with or without a positive decision on their applications, will likely be expected to remit money home or to family and friends elsewhere in the diaspora.

Asylum seekers are portrayed in very different ways by different constituencies. Pro-asylum nongovernment organisations (NGOs), many of which are church-based, and in the UK are encouraging the use of the term 'sanctuary' rather than asylum, emphasise in their public education the 'refugeeness' of the asylum-seeker as someone who it is assumed has arrived in the country of exile immediately from a situation of danger and who is in a bureaucratic process that demands they prove the risk of harm. In so doing, NGOs write out the personal migration history of the individual, the choices made, the decisions taken and indeed the risks of migration. It is understandable that advocates would present the refugee narrative in such a way because the complicated journey to asylum, typically involving periods of time spent in countries other than the country of final asylum, confuses the legal case where people have passed through safe countries but opted to move on. This simpler narrative of danger, flight and sanctuary is also preferred because it is used to counter an alternative and wide held view, in many western countries, that asylum seekers, or at least the case they present, is 'bogus' and the individual is illegal in the sense that their testimonies involve known deception designed to mislead officials responsible for determination and decision making. Evidence from the UK shows that scepticism about the rectitude of asylum claimants features strongly in parts of the tabloid press (Smart et al., 2007) and in times of recession and cut backs in government spending, support to asylum seekers finds ready resentment particularly in those parts of the country where public resources are under pressure and jobs hard to find.

There are then two main competing narratives around asylum seekers, there is the simplified 'refugeeness' of the individual, and the second of the individual as a migrant making rational choices which in themselves are likely to involve illegal acts. Neither of these constructs tells the entire story. The issue of illegality raises particularly difficult moral and ethical issues for researchers. Few academics in the refugee studies field have been prepared to investigate and write about this dimension of asylum seeking. There is a fear of being branded anti-asylum and anti-migration and most social scientists engaged in this field of research would probably describe themselves as being on the political left, inclined to support the preservation of the Refugee Convention and the institution of asylum which they believe is under attack from governments across Europe and in Australia who increasingly employ a global security rationale to restrict access to asylum. Such sensitivity on the part of researchers, reinforced by the labelling of refugees and migrants as vulnerable in some ethics review processes, may however be misplaced. Dauvergne has argued that the laws designed to manage global migration are in themselves constructing illegality (2007, p. 4). Western asylum systems operate in such a way that they will only consider an application for asylum once an individual has arrived at an airport or has reported to a police station or a solicitor and makes a request for asylum. The pursuit of credibility in the asylum case then begins but is only concerned with events that took place in the country of origin and which provide the evidence of persecution and the basis of a protection claim. Governments, in the same way as advocacy NGOs, erase from the record, and in so doing decline to accept responsibility, for the journey that brought a claimant from Somalia across African borders, into the hands of smugglers, through the Mediterranean, across Western Europe to an English Channel port and the packing cases of a container bound for Dover. But as Dauvergne has argued it is precisely these unmanaged, undocumented movements that should be at the centre of asylum research because it is here that human rights violations are most likely to occur, and it is an area that states may be content remains relatively unexplored because it is in this dangerous liminality that a little sovereignty is claimed back as borders are protected. It is argued then that in relation to asylum as a field of research, the dangers of imposing a 'refugeeness' onto asylum seekers with its accompanying assumption of vulnerability should be resisted for two reasons. First, because it closes the door on research about agency in asylum migration; and second, because it elides a proper discussion about the intersection of migration and refugee law and practice and human rights in the context of global protection.

'Environmental Refugees'

The largest group of migrants who have been reclassified as refugees in recent years have been displaced, or are likely to be displaced, by various processes described collectively as environmental change. These include people displaced by rapid onset natural disasters (such as earthquakes and floods), slow onset change (such a desertification, gradual land degradation and crop losses), pollution and land spoiling arising out of industrial processes (burst dams, poisonous emissions), and over the past decade a new category of 'climate refugees' has been added to include those whose lives and livelihoods are at risk principally from projected sea level rise and more erratic weather associated with increased carbon dioxide concentrations and forced global warming. Many millions of people affected by natural disasters, according to the International Committee of the Red Cross (ICRC), receive assistance from the organisation and although the ICRC does not count the number of people displaced in any disaster situation[3], it can be assumed that the majority of those receiving assistance have been displaced. Predictions about climate change created displacement foresee hundreds of millions of people being displaced each year if temperatures continue to rise as modelled (Christian Aid, 2007; Stern Review, 2006; see also McDowell & Morrell, 2010, pp. 55–58).

A number of commentators (Black, 2001; Castles, 2002; McDowell & Morell, 2010) have questioned the very notion of 'environmental refugees'. Legal scholars argue that a refugee is a very specific category of person in international law, someone who has lost state protection and cannot return home for fear of persecution or other harm, and retaining the integrity of this legal definition is vital if meaningful protection is to be provided (Hathaway, 2007). Academics such as Black, Castles and Kibreab (1997) are sceptical about the label because it presupposes a direct single causality between an environmental event (increased temperatures, drought, floods) and human migration. Instead they argue that the migration process is far more complex. Individuals, families and sometimes whole communities make decisions about migration (when, to where, how) in the context of multiple drivers (available resources, policies that affect their decision making, knowledge, opportunity, etc.) and evidence shows that changed environmental conditions (such as drought, or degradation linked to overcrowding or forest depletion) do not automatically lead to migration as people may, depending on a range of other factors, remain in place to ride out the crisis and invest for the future. The deployment of the term 'environmental refugee' by lobbyists, environmental organisations, and indeed governments, should be understood as a political statement at a time in which governments are anxious to carry the public with them as they pursue strategies designed to decarbonise their economies and provide aid to developing countries enabling them to adapt to and mitigate against the impacts of climate change. The label 'refugee' is useful in this regard because it is evocative, it captures the sense of urgency and immediacy, and when coupled with hydrological language ('a tsunami/flood/wave of climate change refugees') it hints none too subtly at public concern over uncontrolled migration, the need to forestall such movements and to further protect borders against incursions. The label serves a further purpose in relation to the international response to environmental crises.

The presence of refugees signals an emergency situation triggering the standard response to displacement, which is to build a refugee camp. In the case of the Dadaab Camp in Kenya, a large extension was added to the camp in preparation for a predicted rise in environmental displacement in the Horn of Africa, linked to ongoing civil war, and in mid 2011 the displaced began arriving at the gates of the camp.

Opposition to the use of the term 'environmental refugee' is therefore largely on legal grounds (the Refugee Convention cannot apply in the overwhelming majority of cases of environmental displacement unless it can be shown that disasters or change combined with conflict was a driver of displacement), on political grounds (to the extent that the label is employed for tactical reasons) and on empirical grounds (the simple causality it suggests between event and displacement/migration is not supported by available evidence). In terms of research ethics there are additional considerations. It is certainly the case that in some natural disasters displaced people find themselves in refugee-like situations. Cyclone Nargis that struck Myanmar/Burma in May 2008 left tens of thousands dead and hundreds of thousands displaced. It was a feature of the response to the crisis that for some weeks after the cyclone hit, the Burmese junta refused to allow the delivery of international aid, citing sovereignty and fear of military invasion, with the effect that the human costs escalated. Walter Kaelin, formerly the Special Representative of the UN Secretary General on the Rights of Internally Displaced Persons has written about the human rights violations that occur in natural disasters (Kaelin, 2005). However, for the overwhelming majority of people displaced by natural disasters the displacement is relatively short term, it occurs within the borders of their state, and they remain under the protection of their government.

Certainly it is the case that even in democratic and wealthy states (as exemplified in Hurricane Katrina in the US in 2005) responses to natural disasters very often fall short and are thought to reveal structural discrimination in societies resulting in the unfair distribution of resources and the political neglect of certain communities (Allen, 2007). But the emergency response is part of the wider political process, authorities can be held to account, and the displaced have the sympathy of the population at large and of the international community which generally commits to global appeals for financial aid. Unlike conflict refugees, victims of natural disasters retain a higher degree of autonomy and have greater control over important decisions affecting their return and reconstruction. For conflict or Convention-status refugees, particularly in civil wars where fighting takes place among the people, displacement is a deliberate strategy to clear areas, alter the ethnic balance and it prepares the way for combatants to control territory and resources. For many conflict refugees returning home is likely to mean return to another location, or if they are able to return to their home towns and villages, much that was previously familiar and secure is likely to have changed, including political and leadership structures and control of land. While return home may not be an option for people whose homes and lands have been destroyed by floods, volcanoes or earthquakes, the prospect of livelihood improvement and livelihood security and the risk of political marginalisation is of a different order for environmental migrants than it is for conflict refugees.

Development Refugees

A final category of displaced people to which the label refugee has been attached, and with it an assumption of 'refugeeness' and being in a 'refugee-like situation', are the 12 to 15 million people who each year lose their homes, lands and livelihoods as a result of development processes designed to boost a nation's economic growth. The bulk of this displacement is taking place in fast industrialising countries such as China, India, Indonesia, and Brazil as a consequence of projects in five main sectors water and hydro power, transport, urban upgrading, the creation of industrial zones, and through policies designed to take people off the land and shift them from agricultural to industrial production. An additional related category of displacement arises out of state resettlement programs, for example, in Ethiopia where large scale resettlement from the Central Highlands to western parts of the country is part of the strategy of land rationalisation ostensibly to reduce overcrowding and boost food production (Hammond, 2008; Pankhurst & Piguet, 2009). A further emerging trend in policy driven displacement is linked to the growing number of climate change adaptation and mitigation projects in the developing world. Drawing on the promised $30 to $100 billion of so called Fast Start aid for climate change investments, governments in Asia, Africa and Latin America and proposing afforestation/reafforestation, new hydro-schemes, coastal defences and biofuel production which will require the acquisition and change of use of millions of hectares of land and necessitate additional involuntary resettlement over the coming decades (McDowell, 2011).

Cernea and McDowell (2000) compared the experiences of development-induced displacement and involuntary resettlement with conflict-induced displacement and concluded that there are parallels but these are principally related to the socioeconomic impacts of asset loss that affect both groups of displaced people. However, in a broader sense, examining issues of security and human rights, there are significant differences. With important exceptions, such as land grabbing and politically-motivated population dispersal (such as that witnessed in Zimbabwe in 2005–2006 under the so called Operation Murambatsvina urban clearances), development-created displacement occurs as part of a legal process which sees states exercising their right of eminent domain to acquire land from private or community ownership which is then used for projects in the national interest. A legal process needs to be gone through in which people are informed of the act of taking land and other assets, frequently there are public hearings and objections, assets have to be valued and compensation payments agreed. The acquisition has to take place within a prescribed period of time and compensation monies paid or replacement land provided.

Where states cannot justify acquisition in the national interest, or they fail to comply with laws and policies, then the actions may be deemed arbitrary[4] or illegal. Unfortunately, it has been widely documented (Bennett & McDowell, 2012; McDowell, 1996) that states, banks and businesses, and international financing organisations such as the multilateral development banks (see, for example, the investigations undertaken by the independent Inspection Panel of the World Bank) who are involved in this process frequently fail to comply with their legal obligations. Research has shown how, for the majority of development-displacees the experience of asset loss and relocation results in deepened impoverishment and marginalisation. Force is often employed to remove populations who resist or oppose land acquisition, and the axe of displacement falls unevenly on minority populations who live in remote areas, may not have legal title to land, and whose livelihoods, on the periphery of the mainstream economy, are particularly vulnerable to the loss of natural and commonly owned resources.

While the record on the involuntary resettlement of people who find themselves in the way of 'development' and 'progress' is poor, and the legal and policy framework is weak and ineffective in protecting affected populations, the extension of the refugee label should be used very cautiously. State authorities have a legal obligation not to disadvantage people who lose assets and the stated purpose of a project that involves land acquisition is an improvement in the human condition. The displaced have not crossed an international border but rather remain full citizens of the state and enjoy state protection. Except in very rare cases they are not encamped or dependent upon humanitarian aid, and indeed for many, the process of involuntary resettlement draws people inextricably into an engagement with, and frequently in conflict with, for the first time, a state and official politics. Though not an engagement of their choosing, political incorporation becomes unavoidable. Certainly it is the case that in states that do not respect the rights of their citizens and where laws are weak or are not upheld, the forced relocation of people, justified on the basis of national gain, can be used as a cover for oppression by governments or by private interests; however such actions are taken outside of eminent domain laws and should be regarded as extra-legal and criminal.

Implications for Ethical Research

It has been shown that while there are commonalities in the displacement experience, whether the proximate cause is conflict, environmental change or development, the assumption that all those displaced are in a refugee-like situation and face the same constraints on autonomy, choice and agency as experienced by encamped refugees is brought into question. Rather, it is argued that the research context and therefore any ethical implications need to be considered for each context. This final section of the chapter will reflect on the particular circumstances of asylum seekers and consider the kinds of ethical safeguards that might be appropriate in relation to confidentiality and research among those detained in the asylum process.

Conducting ethical research among asylum seekers involves significant challenges. Research may take place at any point in what Black and Koser (1999) refer to as the 'refugee cycle': immediate flight, crossing borders in transit, lying low while waiting for an opportunity to move on, in detention or 'holding'/migration processing centres, in an administrative system applying for status or in the courts appealing a decision, in immigration detention pending removal, being removed, on return to country of origin, resettlement in country of origin. Uppermost among ethical considerations is confidentiality. Information is at the heart of asylum decision-making and within the adversarial process disputes about the accuracy and veracity of information relating to events that may have occurred some years previously dominate the process. A final decision on a case can, and frequently does, rest on small pieces of information (Was a village attacked on the 29 or 30 August?, Were the attackers wearing blue or green uniforms?) that are constantly re-examined in an adversarial contest over credibility. Governments draw on significant resources to compile and manage country information that is used by their lawyers and referred to by judges in determination. Asylum applicants by contrast are required to prepare a defence of their claim with far fewer resources and what information is available to them will be guarded with considerable care. Second, asylum seeking for many involves illegality at some level (crossing borders without documentation, procuring false documents or discarding passports, using false names, paying for the services of a smuggler) and for this reason asylum seekers are often reluctant research subjects preferring not to disclose information in case it prejudices their application.

The safeguarding of information in research is therefore critical and preserving the anonymity of the interviewee is vital. It is important that researchers are transparent in explaining the purpose of their research and measures that will be taken to assure confidentiality. Asylum seekers are far more likely to participate in research if the researcher can exhibit a close working knowledge of asylum procedures and moreover an awareness about the use and sensitivity of information in those procedures. In this way a relationship of confidence can be established; ignorance of these matters will reduce the likelihood of cooperation. The author of this chapter has supervised a number of student research projects among those seeking asylum in Europe, and in most cases researchers choose, or are required, to access interviewees through asylum support NGOs who provide assistance. As is the case in northern France around the port of Calais, where voluntary organisations run hostels and feeding centres, access to asylum seekers is strictly managed and the prevailing attitude is one of distrust. Even statistical information (the numbers of people who attend drop-in sessions, their nationalities and ages, their intended destination, migration history) is rarely disclosed. Under such conditions verbal consent is usually preferred to written consent.

Asylum seekers in most European countries, unless they have gone underground to avoid detection by the state, are obliged to remain close to state authorities, reporting regularly to immigration or police officials, renewing documentation, and appearing in legal hearings. Detention is commonly employed as an administrative mechanism by the state and it presents additional ethical implications for research. Asylum seekers in detention have mostly reached the end of the legal process and face imminent deportation. Authorities will likely be reluctant to permit research access as detention tends to be controversial and detainees faced with the trauma of return will go to extraordinary lengths including abuse of the body to draw attention to their cause. Research under such conditions demands more stringent ethical safeguards. While detained asylum seekers as 'captive subjects' are attractive to researchers their autonomy and privacy is impaired. The US Institute of Medicine (2006, p. 3), considering research in prisons, has commented that 'the myopic emphasis on informed consent…should be abandoned in favor of a risk-benefit paradigm'. From this author's experience of conducting research on behalf of the UK Law Society in four British immigration detention centres justifying research on the basis of benefit is particularly problematic because individuals have very little to gain from research given their upcoming removal and with little inclination towards altruism for those who may follow them. Feeding back the results of the research, or corroborating the interpretation of the interview material may not be possible as returnees are difficult to trace on return; an assessment of benefit is therefore a major challenge for institutional review bodies.

In conclusion, this chapter has argued that research among displaced people carries the potential risk of harm to all engaged in the research process and ethics review procedures are vital in predicting those risks and putting in place safeguards that both minimise harm and promote the kind of research that has positive outcomes. However, the current trend, emerging in part out of an approach influenced by an application of the precautionary principle, is to extend the notion of refugeeness encapsulating the real vulnerability of refugees in camps to all categories of displaced people including many migrants. The author of this chapter has argued that review bodies must pay particular attention to research that is conducted in both refugee camps and in places of immigration detention as these are locations where unethical or ill thought through research could have immediate and detrimental impacts on forced migrants and returnees. It is also a contention of the author that researchers and those charged with ethics review must also show awareness of the capacity for independent action and decision making on the part of migrants, the differential levels of legal protection afforded to displaced persons depending on the cause of their displacement and the responses of states and the international bodies, and the potential for political and other forms of resistance that displaced and migrant populations exercise.

Notes

1. Including ethics committee representation at Macquarie University, Sydney, and King's College London and City University London in the UK.
2. See for example the joint activities of the UNHCR and the International Organisation of Migration (IOM) to identify and remove from Libya foreign workers caught up in the fighting to depose Colonel Gadaffi from power in 2011.
3. It is interesting to note that the ICRC has resisted attempts, in particular through the recent development of the so-called 'cluster approach' to humanitarian responses, to use the fact of displacement as a proxy for vulnerability and humanitarian need. The organisation instead argues that people who remain behind, who cannot or choose not to move, may be equally vulnerable and directing attention disproportionately to the displaced may skew resources and leads to new 'protection gaps'.
4. See in particular the definition of arbitrary in the UN Guiding Principles on Internal Displacement.

References

Allen, T.D. (2007). Katrina: Race, class and poverty, reflections and analysis. *Journal of Black Studies, 37*(4), 466–468.

Bennett, O. & McDowell, C. (2012). *Displaced: The human cost of development and resettlement*, New York, NY: Palgrave Macmillan.

Black, R. (2001). Fifty years of refugee studies: From theory to policy. *International Migration Review, 35*(1), 57–78.

Black, R. (2001). Environmental refugees: Myth or reality? *New Issues in Refugee Research (Working Paper No. 34)*. Geneva, Switzerland: UNHCR.

Black, R. & Khoser, K. (Eds.). (1999). *The end of the refugee cycle*, Oxford, England: Berghahn Books.

Castles, S. (2002). Environmental change and forced migration: Making sense of the debate, *New Issues in Refugee Research (Working Paper No. 70)*. Geneva, Switzerland: UNHCR.

Caplan, P. (Ed.). (2003). *The ethics of anthropology: Debates and dilemmas*. London, England: Routledge.

Cernea, M. & McDowell, C. (Eds.). (2000). *Risks and reconstruction: The experiences of resettlers and refugees*, Washington DC: World Bank.

Christian Aid. (2007, May). *Human tide: The real migration crisis*. London, England: Author.

Dauvergne, C. (2007). *Making people illegal: What globalization means for migration and law*. Cambridge, England: Cambridge University Press.

Deng, F. (1996). *Sovereignty as responsibility: Conflict management in Africa*. Washington, DC: Brookings Institution Press.

Duffield, M. (2007). *Development, security and unending war: Governing the world of peoples*. London: Polity Press.

Furedi, F. (2011). *On tolerance: A defence of moral independence*. London, England: Continuum.

Hammond, L. (2008). Strategies of invisibilization: How Ethiopia's resettlement programme hides the poorest of the poor. *Journal of Refugee Studies, 21* (4), 517–536.

Harrell-Bond, B. (1986). *Imposing aid: Emergency assistance to refugees*. Oxford, England: Oxford University Press.

Hathaway, J. (2007). Why refugee law still matters. *The Melbourne Journal of International Law, 8* (1), 89–103.

Institute of Medicine. (2006). *Ethical considerations for research involving prisoners*. Washington DC: Author.

James, W. (2007). *War and survival in Sudan's frontierlands: Voices from the Blue Nile*. Oxford, Egnaldn: Oxford University Press.

Kaelin, W. (2005). *Protection of internally displaced persons in situations of natural disasters*. Washington DC: Brookings Institution.

Kibreab, G. (1997). Environmental causes and impact of refugee movements: A critique of the current debate. *Disasters, 21* (1), 20–38.

Kneebone, S. (2007). A Mediterranean solution? *Around the Globe, 3*(3), 37–39.

Lindley, A. (2010). *The early morning phone call: Somali refugees' remittances*. New York, NY: Berghahn Books.

McDowell, C. (1996). *A Tamil asylum diaspora: Sri Lankan migration, politics and change in Switzerland*. Oxford, England: Berghahn Books.

McDowell, C. (2006). Displacement, return and justice in the creation of Timor Leste. In C. McDowell, & N. Van Hear (Eds.), *Catching fire: Containing complex displacement in a volatile world*. Lanham, ML: Lexington Books.

McDowell, C. (2011). Climate change adaptation and mitigation: Implications for land acquisition and population relocation. London, England: Foresight Programme.

McDowell, C. & Eastmond, M. (2002). Transitions, state-building and the 'residual' refugee problem: The East Timor and Cambodian repatriation experience. *Australian Journal of Human Rights, 8*(1), 7–27.

McDowell, C. & Morrell, G. (2010). *Displacement beyond conflict: Challenges for the 21st Century*. Oxford, England: Berghahn Books.

Pankhurst, A. & Piguet, F. (Eds.). (2009). *Moving people in Ethiopia: Development, displacement and the state*. London, England: James Currey.

Shore, C. (2008). Audit culture and illiberal governance: Universities and the politics of accountability. *Anthropological Theory, 8*(3), 278–298.

Smart, K., Grimshaw, R., McDowell, C., & Crosland, B. (2007). *Reporting asylum: Results of a media monitoring study, analysing the portrayal of asylum seekers and refugees in the UK national, regional and faith/minority press, during January – March 2005*. London, England: Information Centre about Asylum and Refugees.

Stern, N. (2007). *The economics of climate change: The Stern Review*. Cambridge, England: Cambridge University Press.

Vogler, P. (2006). In the absence of the humanitarian gaze: refugee camps after dark. New Issues in Refugee Research (*Working Paper No. 137*). Geneva, Switzerland: UNHCR.

■ ■ ■ ■   ■   ■   ■ ■

CHAPTER

5

The Ethical Implications of the Researcher's Dominant Position in Cross-Cultural Refugee Research

Marinella Marmo

This chapter aims to explore the role of the criminology researcher who seeks to conduct qualitative and ethical research with refugees in crisis conditions. It is argued that the researcher already promotes, albeit in an implicit manner, an ethical agenda aimed at minimising potential harm and protecting individual rights at a macro level. In this, there is an attempt at reshaping the narrative of deviance imposed by those in power on powerless and voiceless asylum seekers. And yet, the same researcher is in a dominant position at a micro level, while conducting research directly with the research subject. In both circumstances, the researcher is imbued with epistemological and ontological orientations, and operates in a historically and ideologically informed context. However, at a micro level, the researcher interacting with refugees in a crisis situation is in a clear dominant position, furthering postcolonial sociopolitical discourse on powerful versus powerless.

The protection of the rights of the research subjects, a key area of concern for research ethics, may add to the political agenda and dominant position of the researcher. It is argued that research ethics in this field of study may be used as a canvas that researchers can stretch to fit their purposes and needs, a tool that we mould to fit our research aims. In this process, the researcher acquires even more political domain over a supposedly objective research agenda, and becomes an even more powerful agent. Knowledge becomes power used as commodity (Smith, 2005).

Discovering knowledge to explore, assess and evaluate complex situations is still the fundamental job of the researcher. It is understandable that when we see human suffering we feel the need to intervene, but this may come at a cost: the researcher's tasks and level of involvement are different from the work of nonprofit organisations, intergovernmental bodies such as the UN refugee agency, social workers and journalists. The implementation of a research project that respects ethical frameworks should complement, not obstruct, the role of the researcher.

This chapter aims to add to more recent research on avoiding or minimising harm (e.g., Hugman, Pittaway, & Bartolomei, 2011; Mackenzie, McDowell, & Pittaway, 2007) at the micro level, and specifically with reference to the interaction between a dominant researcher and a weaker research subject in the destination country. The assumption here is based on the fact that where the refugee is, for example, an unauthorised migrant (such as unauthorised boat arrivals and asylum seekers in mandatory detention centres), it is imperative for the researcher to access the refugee in crisis conditions. The argument proposed is based on the refugee being in a weaker position compared to the (western, probably white) chief investigator.

Nevertheless, it is proposed that the researcher who interacts with the research subject in an ethical manner should not necessarily aim to alleviate suffering (Turton, 1996) or to produce direct outcomes for participants, unless cautionary steps are considered (Mackenzie et al., 2007). In fact, these elements may add to the research agenda, and compromise even further its epistemological and ontological orientations. Taking inspiration from Smith (2005), this chapter argues that the qualitative research conducted by social scientists on refugees in crisis conditions should be ethical and respectful of the fragile party, but not turn the project into social activism. As pointed out by Düvell, Triandafyllidou, and Vollmer (2010, pp. 230–231):

> The researcher is commonly faced with people suffering harsh living and working conditions, and this may well raise ethical dilemmas such as ... the need to intervene.

Turton's objective of alleviating suffering adds to the researcher's political agenda as an 'aim'. And while Turton's objective is justified in terms of ethical standards, of protection of the research subjects, it does stretch the role of academics. Furthermore, this type of research seems embedded in the artificial dichotomy of victim-offender — discussed in the next section.

The dilemma rests in the impossible position of the researcher. Academics seem to be pushed to produce research that has some impact on the real world in terms of protecting refugees and being policy-relevant, as well as aiming 'to satisfy high academic standards' (Jacobsen & Landau 2003, p. 186). This 'dual imperative' is difficult to reconcile at micro level.

The Polarised Debate: Victim-Offender

The status of victim or offender is a social construct (Green, 2007). This is more so in the case of refugees such as those unauthorised boat arrivals and asylum seekers in mandatory detention centres, whose victimhood status is either idealised or rejected. It is idealised when the victim is qualified in terms of fragility, naivety and powerlessness. And yet, to be seen as a victim, a refugee may need to fit not only with some characteristics identified as naïve and weak, but as law-abiding and respectable too (Christie, 1986). These social conditions, according to some mainstream media and political groups, are simply not met; asylum seekers are mostly portrayed, in the destination country, as problematic, and their status of vulnerability questioned. To stratify this argument further, within the conservative ideology of victimhood, those who find themselves in a status of victimhood are believed to be responsible for it (Karmen, 2007). A victim radical stand would reject this notion and identifies broader factors (Mawby & Walklate, 2002), such as global forces and territorial divisions. Yet, the neo-liberal society abides by this conservative-strand notion of personal responsibility (O'Malley, 2004). As Green (2007, p. 91) points out the attributes of the ideal victims are intrinsic: asylum seekers find themselves in condition of need because they have placed themselves in such a position in the first place.

Furthermore, in the way they are portrayed by some politicians and the media, refugees can project a rather different image, such as, being complicit with smugglers (Grewcock, 2009). This negative view is so strongly portrayed that groups of refugees becomes indistinguishable, and blurs those who have waited years in refugee camps with those negatively tagged as 'queue-jumpers'.

A refugee loses the element of vulnerability also because they are portrayed as taking action, losing the passivity element of the typically defined genuine victim (such as an elderly person or a child (Christie, 1986)). Worse, the action taken by refugees, for example, to flee their home countries to shape a better future, is portrayed as an action *against* the interest of the destination country. This is evident in the policy debate concerning refugees in Australia (Grewcock, 2010), where any action that refugees take, for instance forms of protest in mandatory detention centres, are seen as contributing to the cause of constructing the refugee outside the scheme of 'victimhood'.

The case of lip sewing is particularly exemplary to this discussion. Lip sewing was reported as occurring in 2002 among some refugees at the Woomera Detention Centre in South

Australia in protest against their voiceless position while in mandatory detention. Pugliese (2002) reports that Philip Ruddock, the former Minister for Immigration, distanced himself from these episodes claiming that:

> Lip sewing is a practice unknown in our culture. It's something that offends the sensitivities of Australians. The protesters believe it might influence the way we might respond. It can't and it won't (in Pugliese, 2002, s. 5)

The construction of refugee as 'other' and alien to Australian culture helps with the identification of their actions as offending behaviours, more typical of the actions of criminals than victims. Pugliese (2002, s. 40) argues:

> these acts are generated out of Australian soil. Lip sewing is a product of 'our' culture: we produce it legislatively, juridically and penally. The apparatuses of government and law, in their treatment of refugees, extort violence and barbarism from the body of the refugee.

And yet, in the hierarchy of victimhood (Carrabine, Cox, Lee, South, & Plummer, 2009, p. 160), a hierarchy based on the controversial argument that some victims are more innocent than others, if ever asylum seekers make an appearance, it is at the lowest ranks. More than that, cultural forces shape the label of asylum seeker into a 'deviant'.

The result is a moral conflict between the label of 'victim' and the label of 'offender'. The powerful agencies in authority refuse the overlapping figure of a victim-offender or offender-victim, as the two categories are socially constructed as polarised. This confirms the traditional conception of victim and offender as separate and distinct categories (Quinney, 1970). Therefore, if a refugee is seen as not deserving the status of victim, this subject has to be kept in a restrained condition. This is not just physical constraints, as it has broader implications: it contributes to the narrative of criminalisation of the undeserving refugee (Grewcock, 2010). Therefore, 'guilt' is placed within the undeserving subject, and the state is constructed as having no responsibility for the current status quo. The 'apparatuses of government and law' contribute to framing 'the structural prohibition of owning our responsibility' (Pugliese, 2002, s. 41), placing the responsibility back into refugees' hands.

The very fact that we accept, or have not opposed sufficiently strongly against mandatory detention for those cases which are not in breach of criminal law, is a clear sign that we have agreed, as a society[1], to see a refugee through the lens of an insubordinate, noncompliant, alien subject, rather than a victim. In summary, we construct the 'criminal other', and this justifies their treatment as 'criminal'.

The controlling authority has stripped the person of their identity, labelled them as not a deserving subject, and exercised their authority to take away status and power from the person. The lesser status means that the refugee becomes voiceless and cannot contest the level and degree of authority imposed on him/her.

The Position of the Researcher

In this highly politicised environment, the social science researcher enters the research field. There is no denial that within the discipline of critical criminology, the unauthorised migrant, the refugee in crisis condition, is discussed in terms of violation of human rights (Grewcock, 2009; Pickering, 2005). Critical criminologists, such as Pickering and Grewcock, for example, have highlighted the responsibility of the state, and have pushed the discourse even further by considering the action of the state as deviant. It is noted, in the field of critical criminology, that the researcher entering this field does identify the asylum seeker as the voiceless victim party, and aims to become the voice of the refugees' unheard stories. The ethical response of this position can be classified as multidimensional. I will limit this analysis to the micro and macro dimensions. The micro-level response, the direct relationship with the research subject, invokes comprehensive considerations about ethical principles, such as how to minimise the potential for harm, and maximise benefits for the research subject. This part will be discussed in more detail in the next section, and it will be pointed out that the researcher is in the dominant position, potentially adding to an already harmful condition. If the research agenda is mainly outcome driven (for instance, to add to public discourse on victimhood), this may have negative ethical implications.

Here, I aim to discuss the macro dimension, which has been a major point of discussion in criminology. The government and media response to refugees in crisis conditions, especially unauthorised boat arrivals and mandatory detention, has exacerbated even further the dichotomy victim-offender. And in this environment, criminologists such as Grewcock (2009) have attempted to re-balance the discussion by pointing out how the Australian government has played a central role in constructing asylum seekers in negative terms by legitimising punitive border control measures. In this, the field of critical criminology has positioned itself in a substantive standpoint in defence of the refugee. That means that the political agenda of the researcher is filled with the aim to identify the state responsibilities, to point out how the government has created or certainly exacerbated 'the problem' of unauthorised boat arrivals. This standpoint has never been phrased as having ethical implications. I take this occasion to argue that, by embracing the view that the state has abused their powers to compromise asylum seekers' basic human rights, those critical criminologists, such as the ones mentioned above, have put forward a strong ethical position at the macro level. This response is ethical because it promotes the goals of minimising the harm and promoting justice. It is evident the aim of pointing the finger at the responsibilities of the state finds its justification in the identification of the harm caused by the destination country on the refugee. This 'harm' at this macro level is also the manufacture of the refugee's deviance with the scope of seeking to exclude them as unwanted subjects. In this rests the most powerful ethical intervention of critical criminology in this field. The law-abiding and law-breaking behaviours are usually identified through a top-down process performed by the powerful (the state identifies what is wrong and who is deviant). By arguing that the state is the one abusing their powerful position by fabricating and legitimising law-breaking behaviours — otherwise not-recognised as such by international agreements — there is an attempt to shape a different narrative aimed to promote justice and reduce harm.

The next section argues that the researcher, the criminologist that positions himself/herself between the asylum seeker and the state, from the relative powerless position towards the state, becomes the dominant party in the researcher–research subject relationship. The problems addressed next aim to contextualise at the micro level the researcher's scope. I should point out that the powerless-powerful paradigm discussed in critical criminology at macro level has explicit and constructive ethical implications. However, when we revert back to the micro dimension we face a reverse of roles, where the powerful is the researcher.

The Researcher as Dominant Party

Following from the discussion in the previous section, it is evident that the critical criminologist would consider that the refugee in crisis conditions is the powerless party, positioning his/her arguments in open conflict with some media and political statements. Powerlessness is openly acknowledged, and the researcher takes sides in the victim-offender dichotomy. In this exercise, the researcher often identifies the refugee as the 'victim' of both the destination country's sociopolitical system and of broader negative forces of globalisation. Perhaps the underlying driving force is to rebalance the power between the state and the asylum seekers. Nevertheless, at the micro level, in the relationship between researcher and research subject, the powerless remains the asylum seekers. And the researcher is in the dominant position.

Denzin and Lincoln (2005) highlight that normally the researcher is in a powerful position with respect to the research subject. Because of the dynamics of qualitative research interactions, the researcher portrays and projects a sense of superiority over the research subject. The researcher is also the only one in control of the interpretation of empirical data, even when the research subject is offered to review material. All this has major ethical implications. Furthermore, the researcher dominates the research object/subject because he/she has a specific interest in making the research project 'work', from gaining access to obtaining data. This is mainly aimed at broadening scientific knowledge, but there are other imperatives for furthering the professional agenda, for instance in terms of dissemination of findings, publication, accessing research grants, promotion. Within this, some unethical stories have emerged in social sciences (Adler & Adler, 2001), and more recently in refugee studies, especially regarding careless or malicious disclosure of information (Düvell et al., 2010; Hugman et al., 2011; Mackenzie et al., 2007; Pittaway & Bartolomei, 2003).

To add another element, the researcher is also in a powerful position because the subordination of the research subject in the case of refugees in crisis conditions is even wider, with the refugee being a fragile, voiceless party, and constantly reminded of their victim-offender status. The researcher is (or should be) the informed outsider, who scientifically reads the situation, through the lens of sociopolitical and cultural positioning, and disseminates knowledge to key stakeholders. The researcher becomes the conduit of their voice, and the main gate-keeper of the information gained; this certainly adds to the researcher's power, and has major ethical repercussions. In this instance, it is important to reflect how the researcher's behaviour can aim to minimise harms and promote justice. In this process, it is evident that there are two emerging constraints: the external situation, formed by current and past circumstances, and the internal interaction with the research subject.

The external situation is caught in the historical, ideological and political representation of each element. The construction of the refugee as a nondeserving victim, a 'deviant', denotes a 'hostile political environment in which the rights and needs of refugees are often misrepresented and devalued' (Schweitzer & Steel, 2008, p.94). This environment is a product of symbolic interpretations and constructed knowledge of subjectivity (Said, 1978). The (western, possibly white) researcher is not an abstract entity, but is part of this external context. The researcher, who may walk into the project already as a stronger party as he/she dictates the research agenda, acquires more controlling powers due to those external factors. The researcher does not *become* the dominant party; he/she is the dominant party.

Ethical Boundaries

From a methodological viewpoint, linguistic and sociocultural signifiers, therefore, become central. Cross-cultural research rests in the challenge of finding comparable variables (O'Neill, 1997, p. 141) both for the validity of the data and to align the project to ethical frameworks. How these variables, such as comparable linguistic meanings and or sociopolitical understandings, are chosen is often an exercise that requires reflection on the type of information these variables were apt to disclose, and their homogeneity (see also Mackenzie et al., 2007). From the empirical methodology to the theoretical selection of data, it should be assured that the selected variables can travel together. Nevertheless, despite the many steps we can take to control external constraints, ideological and historical practices may be distorted, and knowledge produced is believed as 'real'. Said (1978) would claim that knowledge has been 'naturalised'. In this way, the researcher dominates the voiceless research subject, and represents their reality — that becomes the only reality (for instance, in the victim-offender dichotomy). From an ethical viewpoint, this is certainly problematic. At this micro level, the researcher is the powerful entity, and even if there is an overall ethical aim to promote justice, the researcher becomes the filter. If ethical research is understood as a way to protect the rights of vulnerable groups, we could query where the limits of this protection should start and end. If the ethical boundaries of protection of the fragile research subject are not designated well in advance and rationalised during and after the data-gathering and analysing process, this adds to the already populated political research agenda. The risk is to try to 'reach out', to promise to 'help' by becoming their — filtered — voice, to be more than a 'researcher' (Smith, 2005), which reflects on the way methodologies are applied in the field, for instance by being (ever more) selective in the choice of research participants. It is urged, therefore, that researchers self-reflect on their role as academics before entering the field, and consider the range of possible direct and indirect outcomes of research studies on the cohort of participants as well as research output, impact and timeframes.

Research as a Cross-Cultural Encounter

The internal relationship, the relationship established between the researcher and the research subject, also offers an array of cross-cultural postcolonial issues, where the researcher dominates the subject, and is seen as belonging to an ethnically or socially privileged group. In the category of vulnerable groups such as refugees, cross-cultural barriers are highly significant. The refugee holds an identity (understood as an aggregate of ethnic and religious background, language, age, gender, socioeconomic and political status) different from the researcher; the characteristics of both researcher and the research subject have an impact on the overall outcome of the research, especially in cases of direct interaction (interviews, observation) with the human subject. Denzin (1998) claims that the way an interview flows is influenced by the race, class, gender and ethnicity of the researcher. This type of nonverbal information constitutes the *first impression* and therefore counts for a lot. Ryen (2003) addresses the importance of both the verbal and non-verbal communication in cross-cultural and cross-national interaction. The researcher should explore means to access the researched community and be accepted. Cross-cultural differences in this category can be minimised by being closely related to the object of research. Jiang, Lambert, and Wang (2006, p. 5) suggest as a possible solution to have a more inclusive research team. It is valuable, they argue, that one person on the research team has a degree of experience and understanding with broader cultural complexities of the research subject. Addressing sociocultural and linguistic signifiers can contribute to minimise the effects of the dominant role. Ethnicity and social status are clearly elements that distinguish the researcher even further as dominant, especially when the interaction takes place in the first language of the researcher or an intermediate is used for interaction.

Even if the researcher pays attention to these elements, the interaction is influenced by the historical and ideological symbolic construction of narratives. The researcher as a visitor or as an intruder does offer ethical problems. Shah (2010) claims that:

> An outsider-interviewer is a visitor on a cross-cultural site, and any emerging constructions of her/his subjectivity by the interviewee/s impact the directions of the interview and the data collected. (p. 567)

Also, if the researcher is strongly identified as dominating the exchange, or if other external factors in the interaction are not taken sufficiently into account (for instance safety or sensitive issues) the participants may offer views that are not necessarily trustworthy (see 'responses barriers' in Jiang et al., 2006), or may be reluctant to share information (Adler & Adler, 2001). The further problem of being the dominant party results in being considered as the solution-finder. The research subject:

can potentially misinterpret the role of the researcher and believe that researchers can positively influence their situation because they are 'powerful'. (Düvell et al., 2010, p. 234)

Being seen as the solution-finder may exacerbate, rather than alleviate, harm and therefore this has further ethical implications. Ethical research means not only receiving informed consent and not harming participants, but also 'not deceiving them about research's aims' (Flick, 2009, p. 37). The research subject, by identifying the researcher as the powerful entity *in charge of* the outcome of the research, will develop an expectation (that sufferance is alleviated). Turton's (1996) position is that research in human suffering is only justifiable if explicitly driven by the aim of redressing such suffering. Turton's premise is that one category of people can be identifiable as 'victims' and, therefore, in need of help. The problem with this lies in the fact that the researcher may select those arguments and people that can fulfil certain requirements that match the research agenda. Finding the middle ground between research agenda and research subject's expectations is challenging, and opens a new way of looking at research ethics. As reflected by Düvell et al. (2010) in the context of a researcher who provided assistance:

> This considerably changed the position of the researcher who became engaged in welfare/social work ... Being prepared for such dilemmas ... striking the balance between research and humanitarian relief became a crucial part of our fieldwork. (p. 234)

If research subjects believe there is a direct outcome for them, it is questionable how they give 'consent', and how their needs, concerns and values are openly shared, rather than filtered in a way to match the researcher's demands. The researcher is in the dominant position, and therefore is the stronger negotiator. As Hugman et al. (2011, p. 8) point out:

> When entering difficult camp situations as white/Western researchers, we have observed that people are so desperate for

any form of assistance that they appear to agree to requests for participation in the hope that we might be able to assist them in some tangible way.

Reciprocity as a Solution?

In this context, reciprocity as a process, pursued as coherently as Mackenzie et al. (2007) suggest, may bring a level of clarity about the positioning of the parties. However, if reciprocity is offered openly (for example, participating in an interview in exchange of some direct benefit), it is questioned whether the researcher–participant relationship would be tampered further. While it is fully recognised that participatory action research may offer numerous benefits,[3] it is clear that it offers some problematic downsides as well. Particularly, it is argued that, if there is an exchange of favours on offer, the researcher is perceived even more as the 'gate-keeper', the person in power, the one with something to offer. This adds to the problem of powerful versus powerless.

And yet, the participatory model understood as collaborative research design may perhaps add a positive element to this discourse. From a criminological angle, the collaborative model was re-proposed (Israel, 2004) in the context of indigenous populations, where parties involved (the researcher and the research subject) design the project and identify its goal mutually. While it is recognised that in the case of refugees in crisis it may be difficult to act upon this, participatory research may offer some advantages as it does address the power-struggle: the negotiation may develop trust; expectations and opportunities (or lack of) for direct outcomes are clearly discussed beforehand. Further to this, Schweitzer and Steel (2008) highlight that trust is fundamental, and relationships may be reciprocal in terms of, for instance, hospitality rather than direct benefits. It is suggested that, as reciprocity, participatory and collaborative research are emerging areas in the field of refugee study, a comprehensive and external evaluation of the different studies could be performed, as it may add some original knowledge in the area of the positioning of the researcher as well as their researcher's agendas before, during and after the data-gathering process.

It should be also noted that institutions of control (such as ethics committees) may just add to the postcolonial discourse of powerful *versus* powerless. Placed between the external constraints and internal constraints, the institutions of control are supposed to facilitate research that has clear ethical frameworks. As Israel (2004) points out, the ethics committee may not necessarily have awareness of local cultural values.[4] This point is echoed by those researching in refugees studies (see for instance Mackenzie et al., 2007). This is even more problematic when the research subject is vulnerable. Smith (2005) notes that:

> Research ethics is often much more about institutional and professional regulations and codes of conduct than it is about the needs, aspirations, or worldviews of 'marginalized and vulnerable' communities. (p. 96)

Furthermore, codes of ethics are usually established by the dominant society. Universal standards of human rights and code of ethics have been established by powerful mainstream collective entities and have been imposed upon the subject. This adds to stripping power from the research subject, and assigns an even further level of dominance to the researcher. Therefore, the researcher is in a powerful position towards the research subject. Ethics involving ways of thinking that protect the rights and positions of the fragile research subject should also engage with the construction of meanings and power-struggles between subjectivities. A more balanced discussion on critical criminology and ethical implications should engage with these themes. And while I am not in position to offer 'solutions', reconsidering powerful and powerless narratives can add to a more balanced discussion.

Conclusion

Research ethics and refugees in crisis conditions are both topics that have been considered together very recently. Gaining access, gathering data, negotiating exit from the field as well as producing outputs in ethical manner are emergent ways to consider research methods in this field. Research that is ethically driven and scientifically sound is a powerful negotiating tool with policymakers at the macro level.

In the field of refugees in crisis conditions, however, external historical, institutional, cultural and political constraints have pushed the researcher to consider ethical frameworks as a way to reach out and alleviate suffering. Adding moral obligations to the researcher's agenda can compromise the quality of the work produced. Also, the dominant figure of the researcher in this context is a distinct feature that needs to be considered in more detail. The researcher who investigates in this field is the dominant party who represents and filters refugees' reality.

It is recognised therefore that empirical methodologies and cross-cultural research in this field are challenging. Only at a macro level, the critical criminologist can claim that ethical imperatives are addressed. At this level, the criminologist negotiates for harm minimisation and justice outcomes with those powerful governmental bodies that construct the refugee as a generic criminal other. Because of this, this chapter argues that at macro level the criminologist contributes to the ethical agenda. This differs from the micro level, where the dominant position of the researcher is ethically problematic. The researcher should reflect on the boundaries of ethical research very carefully before entering the field, and investigate their positioning, research aims, and limitations.

Notes

1. Refer to Grewcock (2010) and the 2004 Australian High Court case *Behrooz* where the High Court legitimises mandatory detention.
2. But see Olesen (2011) for some counter-arguments regarding the power of the researcher, including being 'partial ... tenuous ... and confused with researcher responsibility' (p.136).

3. A very good example is in Pittaway and Bartolomei (2013), where the exchange was negotiated during a long period, and consisted in human rights training. Another good example is recounted in Düvell et al. (2010, p. 234): 'if the interviewee asked for advice, or to be recommended a lawyer or psychosocial support, we responded'.

4. See Israel (2004) and Israel and Hay (2006) for further discussion around a number of ethical issues for social scientists (namely: confidentiality; informed consent; harms and benefits; research integrity and researcher's relationships). In refugee studies, ethical complexities and vulnerability of refugees have been recently explored in more detail; see for instance: Allotey & Manderson, 2003; Mackenzie et al., 2007; Zwi et al., 2006).

References

Adler, P.A., & Adler, P. (2001). Reluctant respondent. In J.F. Gubrium & J.A. Holstein (Eds.), *Handbook of interview research: context and method* (pp. 515–536) Thousand Oaks, CA: Sage.

Allotey, P., & Manderson, L. (2003). From case studies to casework: ethics and obligations in research with refugee women. In P. Allotey (Ed.), *The health of refugees: Public health perspectives from crisis to settlement.* (pp. 200–211). Melbourne, Australia: Oxford University Press.

Behrooz v Secretary, Department Of Immigration and Multicultural And Indigenous Affairs [2004] HCA 36.

Carrabine, E., Cox, P., Lee, M., South, N., & Plummer, K. (2009). *Criminology: A sociological introduction.* London, England: Routledge.

Christie, N. (1986). The ideal victim. In E. Fattah. (Ed.), *From crime policy to victim policy* (pp. 1–17). London, England: MacMillan.

Denzin, N. (1998). The art and politics of interpretation. In N. Denzin, & Y. Lincoln (Eds.), *Collecting and interpreting qualitative materials* (pp. 313-44). Thousand Oaks, CA: Sage.

Denzin, N., & Lincoln, Y. (2005). Introduction: The discipline and practice of qualitative research. In N. Denzin, & Y. Lincoln (Eds.), *The sage handbook of qualitative research* (pp. 1–32). Thousand Oaks, CA: Sage.

Düvell, F., Triandafyllidou, A., & Vollmer, B. (2010). Ethical issues in irregular migration research in Europe. *Population, Space and Place, 16*, 227–239.

Flick, U. (2009). *An introduction to qualitative research.* London, England: Sage.

Green, S. (2007). Crime, victimisation and vulnerability. In S. Walklate (Ed.), *Handbook of victims and victimology* (pp. 91–118). Cullompton, England: Willan.

Grewcock, M. (2009). *Border crimes: Australia's war on illicit migrants.* Sydney, Australia: Institute of Criminology Press Grewcock, M. (2010). The great escape: Refugees, detention and resistance.University of New South Wales Faculty of Law Research Series 8. *In Proceedings of the State Crime and Resistance Symposium, Victoria University of Wellington, 18-19 January 2010.* New Zealand.

Hugman, R., Pittaway E., & Bartolomei, L. (2011). When 'do no harm' is not enough: The ethics of research with refugees and other vulnerable groups. *British Journal of Social Work, 41*, 1271-1287.

Israel, M., & Hay, I. (2006). *Research ethics for social scientists: Between ethical conduct and regulatory compliance.* London: Sage.

Israel, M. (2004). *Ethics and the governance of criminological research in Australia.* Sydney, Australia: NSW Bureau of Crime Statistics and Research.

Jacobsen, K., & Landau, L. (2003). The dual imperative in refugee research: Some method-ological and ethical considerations in social science research on forced migration. *Disasters, 27*(3), 185–206.

Jiang, S., Lambert E.G. & Wang J. (2006). Issues in cross-cultural criminal justice survey research: A case of U.S. and China collaboration. *Internet Journal of Criminology.*

Karmen, A. (2007). *Crime victims: An introduction to victimology.* Belmont, CA: Wadsworth.

Mackenzie, C., McDowell, C., & Pittaway, E. (2007). Beyond 'do no harm': The challenge of constructing ethical relationships in refugee research. *Journal of Refugee Studies, 20*(2), 299–319.

Mawby, R. I., &Walklate, S. (2002). *Critical criminology: International perspectives.* London, England: Sage.

O'Malley, P. (2004). *Risk, uncertainty and government.* London, England: Glasshouse Press.

Olesen, V. (2011). Feminist qualitative research in the millennium? First decade: Developments, challenges, prospects. In. N. Denzin, & Y. Lincoln (Eds.), *The sage handbook of qualitative research* (pp. 129–146). Thousand Oaks, CA: Sage.

O'Neill, M. (1997). Border crossings: Opportunities and challenges in comparative research. In P. Burnham (Ed.), *Surviving the research process in politics* (pp. 141–49). London, England: Pinter.

Pickering, S. (2005). *Refugees and state crime.* Sydney: The Federation Press.

Pittaway, E., & Bartolomei, L. (2003).*Women at risk field research report: Thailand.* Sydney, Centre for Refugee Research, University of New South Wales.

Pittaway, E. & Bartolomei, L. (2013). Doing ethical research: Whose problem is it anyway? In K. Block, E. Riggs & N. Haslam (Eds.), *Values and vulnerabilities: The ethics of research with refugees and asylum seekers.* Brisbane, Australia: Australian Academic Press.

Pugliese, J. (2002). Penal asylum: Refugees, ethics, hospitality. *Borderlands, 1*(1). Retrieved from http://www.Borderlandsejournal.Adelaide.Edu.Au/Vol1no1_2002/Pugliese.htm

Quinney, R. (1970). *The social reality of crime.* Boston, MA: Little Brown & Co.

Ryen, A. (2003). Cross-cultural interviewing. In J. Holstein & J. Gubrium (Eds.), *Inside interviewing* (pp. 429–448). Thousand Oaks, CA: Sage.

Said, E. W. (1978). *Orientalism.* London, England: Routledge.

Schweitzer, R., & Steel, Z. (2008). Researching refugees: Methodological and ethical con-siderations. In P. Liamputtong (Ed.), *Doing cross-cultural research* — Social Indicators Research Series, (Vol. 34, pp. 87–101).

Shah, S. (2010). The researcher/interviewer in intercultural context: A social intruder! *British Educational Research Journal, 30*(4), 549–575.

Smith, L. (2005). On tricky ground, researching the native in the age of uncertainty. In N. Denzin & Y. Lincoln (Eds.), *The Sage handbook of qualitative research* (pp. 85-107). Thousand Oaks, CA: Sage.

Turton, D. (1996). Migrants and refugees. In T. Allen (Ed.), *In search of cool ground: War, flight, and homecoming in northeast Africa* (pp. 96-110). Trenton, NJ: Africa World Press.

Zwi, A., Grove, N., Mackenzie, C., Pittaway, E., Zion, D., Silove, D. & Tarantola, D. (2006). Placing ethics in the centre: negotiating new spaces for ethical research in conflict sit-uations. *Global Public Health, 1*(3), 264–277.

CHAPTER

6

The Role of Respect in Research Interactions With Refugee Children and Young People

Jeanette A. Lawrence, Ida Kaplan, and Colleen McFarlane

> All human interaction, including the interaction involved in human research, has ethical dimensions. However, 'ethical conduct' is more than simply doing the right thing. It involves acting in the right spirit, out of an abiding respect and concern for one's fellow creatures. (NHMRC, 2007, p. 3).

In this chapter, we focus attention on a specific group of people from refugee backgrounds — children and adolescents. We also focus attention on respect as a guiding principle for researchers' interactions with this group.

The Australian NHMRC gives respect pride of place among its national guidelines for research, claiming explicitly that, 'among these values (i.e., research merit and integrity, justice, beneficence) respect is central' (NHMRC, 2007, p. 11). That prominence is in agreement with other national and international regulatory bodies. Two influential bodies specifically point to universal and protective forms of respect, and these forms are particularly relevant for research involving refugee young people. The Belmont Report (US National Institute of Health, 1979, p. 4) lays down: 'first that individuals should be treated as autonomous agents, and second, that persons with diminished autonomy are entitled to protection'. Similarly, the Council for International Organizations of Medical Sciences (CIOMS, 1993) specifies that:

> those who are capable of deliberation about their personal choices should be treated with respect for their capacity for self-determination', and 'protection of persons with impaired or diminished autonomy, [which] requires that those who are dependent or vulnerable be afforded security against harm or abuse.

We take up these dual forms of respect when referring to the specific conditions of refugee young people as research participants (using 'refugee young people' as our general term throughout). The universal form of respect relates to their basic value as persons and their basic human rights. The protective form of respect involves protection from further harm or abuse for those who have already suffered. To these forms, we also add a beneficial or compensatory form of respect — one that looks to the possibility of carefully constructed research that can make positive contributions to the experiences of refugee young people.

Researchers, policymakers and service providers have much to learn from these young people. How to develop research projects that can obtain their unique insights without exposing them to the risk of further harm, however, is the challenge for researchers and research review committees. The due application of respect in research, we argue, provides the basis of the equitable treatment of young refugee research participants, laying down the researcher's responsibility to recognise their status and value as persons. It also provides a basis for addressing their needs for protection as formerly unprotected young persons still vulnerable to further violation and exploitation, and their needs for the benefits that can flow from respect-driven treatment.

Because of the potential for both positive and negative treatment of these young people, the role of the researcher requires careful attention. Failure to recognise particular needs can become a form of exploitation, as can over-protectionism. We propose respect as the effective guideline for the design, execution and review of ethically appropriate research involving refugee young people.

To address the place of respect in research, this chapter is organised in four sections. The first section sets the scene, introducing the special position of refugee young people as research participants. The second section follows this scene setting with an analysis of respect as a guiding principle for research interactions. This leads to the third section that examines the researcher's responsibility to work out ways to give their young refugee participants due respect. That responsibility can best be fulfilled, we argue in the final section, by interpreting the dimensions of respect and translating those dimensions into action at various decision points in the development and execution of research projects.

Refugee Young People as Potential Research Participants: The Experiences of Refugee Young People

Respect begins with understanding the people to be respected. Refugee young people have suffered traumatising and harmful experiences in various forms and at the hands of adults. Comprising nearly half the world's 15 million refugees, they are among the most vulnerable of the vulnerable. In many cases, it is possible to trace the effects of violations of their rights and personhood through their experiences in their home country, during their flight from destruction and dislocation, and often, well into resettlement in new nations (Goodnow, in press; McFarlane, Kaplan, & Lawrence, 2011; Williams, 2007). Young people's experiences of either deliberate or incidental harm are likely to impact on their early and later development, and make them liable to exploitation in the many settings where they interact with adults both formally and informally.

In their home countries, for example, young people are exposed to war, persecution, torture, loss of loved ones, poverty, and major disruptions to families and community structures. Many live most of their young lives in refugee camps. In the forced move from their homes, young people sometimes are unaccompanied by adults, and sometimes have to take adult roles upon themselves in traumatised and diminished families. Parents may send their children out of danger zones ahead of the family, or become separated from them as they flee. Some young people are picked up and brought along by adults on the move (family or not). Others travel as unaccompanied minors (Bhabba & Crock, 2006; Luster, Quin, Bates, Johnson, & Rana, 2009).

During resettlement in a new country, their personal histories of persecution, violence, displacement, and violations of their human rights can leave young people open to short-term or long-term effects of their trauma and flight (McFarlane et al., 2011). They may encounter new stressors that exacerbate the impact of previous traumatic experiences (e.g., discrimination, language and learning difficulties, poverty, poor nutrition and housing, lack of access to structural resources). These stressors are likely to be exacerbated by other people's misunderstanding of the cultural, social and psychosocial dimensions of young people's interactions (e.g., intercultural conflict, social deprivation, and continuing attachment and identity-related issues; Victorian Foundation for Survivors of Torture: VFST, 1996). It is no surprise, then, that young refugees are liable to experience mental health disorders and symptoms at higher rates than the general population (Fazel, Wheeler, & Danesh, 2005; Lustig et al., 2004). There is ample evidence, then, to count young refugees among those who require special attention when they are asked to participate in research. They are at risk, in Hurst's (2008, p. 195) terms, of 'an identifiably increased likelihood of incurring additional or greater wrong'.

Vulnerability and Susceptibility to Further Harm

Vulnerability is a difficult concept to apply to particular groups, because the process of attribution can reduce a group's already precarious standing in other people's minds. Such reduction, for instance, accompanies any stereotypic allusions to deficit, weakness, or incompetence. Vulnerability has been frequently attributed to research participants in ways that according to Levine, Faden, Grady, Eckenwiler, and Sugarman (2004) can make it difficult to recruit almost any conceivable research participant. Nevertheless, there are some groups (including the young) who by virtue of their lack of power or knowledge are more open to abuse than others. Levine et al. (2004) argue that the vulnerability clause needs revisiting in medical research. It should not be automatically invoked for broad categories of people, even for those who may be seen as especially vulnerable. It also should not be applied exclusively to issues of informed consent. We join them in calling for careful consideration and for greater awareness of what vulnerability may actually mean for some people, calling also for greater attention to matching research methods to participants (Lawrence & Dodds, 2010).

We urge alertness against interacting with refugee young people without due respect for their vulnerable conditions. We also urge alertness against seeing refugee young people only in terms of their displacement and suffering. Many have made successful transitions into new life pathways in their new countries (Correa-Velez, Gifford, & Barnett, 2010). That success, however, and the threat of over-protection do not remove their entitlement to careful consideration of their developmental needs and their lack of control in interactions with professional adults. When the control of the researcher is exploitative, and when research tasks are not well explained or culturally translated or interpreted, the research environment can be particularly intimidating for young people.

The UNHCR (1994, p. 71) specifically linked the vulnerability of refugee children to their developmental needs and their dependence on adults: 'Three interrelated factors contribute to the special needs of refugee children: their dependence, their vulnerability, and their developmental needs (i.e., their requirements for healthy growth and development at different ages)'.

Along with their peers, refugee young people are normatively vulnerable in their dependence on adults (especially, parents and carers) and in their relative powerlessness in interactions with adults in authority positions. All children can be put at physical and psychological risk by adult thoughtlessness, and some by adult exploitation and abuse.

The relative powerlessness of young people is offensive when young people are denied the right to make a contribution to decision-making about their own lives. Parkinson and Cashmore (2008), for instance, report how young people in separated families do not always want to make the ultimate decisions about their placement. They want a voice and a say in the decision. We know of no similar research evidence of the circumstances that make their powerless state particularly offensive to refugee young people.

There are, however, nonnormative, exceptional aspects to the vulnerability of refugee young people. For young people from some nonwestern cultures, for instance, institutionalised powerlessness and voicelessness may take additional forms that are sanctioned by the hierarchical organisation of family life, gender-related roles or religious doctrines and practices (e.g., religiously endorsed paternalism and female subservience). In general, their poor access to community services means that young people coming from war-torn and troubled countries are unlikely to have clear understanding of their rights in their new country. Institutionalised research rights are likely to be foreign concepts. In effect, dependence on adults can place refugee young people at distinct disadvantage. It is hard for them to claim their rights and privileges. That disadvantage is heightened if young people from other cultures attribute authority to a seemingly 'official' adult.

Rather than furthering powerlessness, researchers should see themselves as optimising the voices and self-determination of their young participants. This practice also makes good sense. Research responses are likely to be more authentic and informative, if young participants feel their participation is valued. Past and possible risks do not automatically require prohibitive protectionism or extreme parentalism (of paternal or maternal kinds) on the part of researchers or review committees. What is needed instead is the considered application of respect.

The Role of Respect in Human Interactions

That consideration is grounded in an analysis of the nature of respect, and particularly of its potential effect for good when applied to human interactions.

The Effect of Respect

As we showed initially, respect is prominent among the guiding principles of many bodies that set up and regulate the policies and practices of ethical research (e.g., Belmont Report, 1979; CIOMS, 1993; NHMRC, 2007). In giving respect primacy among the ethical principles, for instance, the NHMRC (2007, p. 11) points to the individualised worth of all potential research participants that 'involves recognising that each human being has value in himself or herself, and that this value must inform all interaction between people'. Dillon (2010) took that general idea deeper into the ability of duly given respect to enhance people's self-respect, and therefore the value they and others see in their lives:

> whether and how people respect or disrespect each other or themselves, are respected or disrespected by others, individually or collectively, are worthy or unworthy of the respect of others or of themselves, significantly shape the moral quality of individuals' lives, their interpersonal interactions, and their social and political organisations and engagements, determining to a significant extent whether individuals flourish or flounder. (p. 18)

Dillon takes the discussion forward to the positive psychological impact that respectful interactions can promote — a vital consideration when working with refugee young people whose prior experiences are unlikely to have promoted their self-respect. Researchers can be actively engaged in assisting their research participants to 'flourish', by enhancing their sense of control and agency. While this consideration may not be at the forefront of every researcher's objectives, consideration of the nature and application of respect can open up the understanding of research interactions to new possibilities.

Dimensions of Respect

At its most basic level, any interaction where respect is given and received is an activity involving two persons. One is the 'Subject' who does the respecting. The other is the 'Object' of that respecting. Although philosophers typically use those terms, we prefer to describe the Subject as the respect*er* and the Object as the respect*ed*. This avoids suggestions of any linguistic objectification of the persons to whom respect is directed.

We draw on several sources to examine the nature and significance of respect — first on philosophical analyses of respect (specifically, Dillon, 1992; 2010), and then on direct applications of respect to research (e.g., Dickert, 2010; Morrow & Richards, 1996; Thompson, 1990). We bring these several analyses together in analysing the role respect plays when working specifically with young refugee research participants. Respect is an effective guide for ethical research interactions because research participants are given their due and value as persons through the respecter's recognition, attitudes, and behaviour.

Recognising the Value of all Persons

While there are differences about the sources of the meanings of respect, much of what has been written about the respect due to all persons goes back to Immanuel Kant (1797/1996). Kant grounded respect in the autonomy of the person as a moral being. Respect is stipulated, for instance, in his categorical imperative that people should always be treated as ends in themselves and never as means to other people's ends.

This stipulation is not controversial when applied to cognitively intact and morally autonomous adults. In principle, they can be treated as moral beings capable of making moral judgements and taking responsibility. They are due respect by virtue of that autonomous state.

It can be readily seen, however, how some commentators question whether respect can be appropriately directed to people who may not be seen as fully sentient or fully autonomous. These questions are concerned mainly with people who are unconscious, demented, mentally disabled, and unfortunately, for some commentators, young. How can these classes of people be seen as autonomous?

John Rawls (1971, p. 505) provided a helpful clarification of this point. Rawls acknowledged that respect is due to a person on the basis of their being a 'moral being', that is, as 'a being with a sense of justice and a concept of good'. He, however, qualified that criterion by allowing that, at least in the case of the young, 'this feature may be potentialities only'. Even though the full capacity of a moral being may not yet be developed, the developing person is to be recognised, and 'to receive the full protection of principles of justice' (p. 509). In this account, young people cannot be excluded from the universal class of moral beings to whom respect is due. Nor can people whose moral sentiments cannot be readily expressed because of cultural or language differences. Valuing people as worthy of respect, then, involves starting with their universal and generic worth as moral beings with at least the potential of being morally autonomous and of being able to convey their moral sentiments if given the appropriate opportunity. This clause places obligations on the giver of respect to make some of those potentials and conditions possible.

Respect as the Due of Specific Persons

Both Dillon (1992) and Dickert (2010) argue strongly that respect needs to go beyond autonomy and into protective criteria. As we have shown, that protective form of respect is acknowledged as an ethical requirement for research (e.g., COIMS, 1993).

All people are entitled to respect — that is the baseline. Over and above that universal valuing, however, respect is differentially offered to people on several bases. Certain people, for example, are given respect because of their character, their status, or their achievements (e.g., monarchs, popular leaders, sportspersons). This extra respect takes the form of adulatory recognition. Others are given respect in response to their experience of difficult circumstances (e.g., people who struggle in the face of great odds, survivors of disasters). This form of respect also can take on a type of celebrity approach. Survivors of disasters can be treated as heroes regardless of what they actually did.

Then there are people who are recognised because they are seen to be the exploited, the powerless, or the vulnerable. These are the people to be offered protective respect in Dillon's (1992, 2010) terms. The respect given to them rarely adds up to adulation or celebrity status. Rather, it is the recognition of the rights of exploited people, especially due to those who have had their personhood denied and now should have it restored. It is likely to involve the giver, the respecter in extra efforts to repair the damage already done. This is the kind of compensatory respect that works towards restoring people's previously denied self-respect.

Dillon (1992), in particular, focused on the tension between treating people equally as moral beings, and treating people differentially — equitably, because of their conditions and circumstances. Drawing on feminist theory, Dillon particularised respect as a response to the person, the whole person, the specific 'me' or 'you' in a given setting. Respecting the violated and the vulnerable, for example, involves paying special attention to the likelihood of attacks on their dignity and wellbeing (Dillon, 2010).

That compensatory aspect of respect, undergirds what Dillon (1992, p. 116) called the special condition of 'care respect'. Care respect is one aspect of responding to people's circumstances. In affirming the protective and caring aspects of respect giving, Dillon also sharply brought to the fore the evaluative, recognition component of respect that is always present, even in its everyday use.

In short, respect carries with it the sense of valuing the respected — of taking people, including young refugee research participants seriously — of seeing them as distinct individuals who cannot be substituted one for another. They cannot be treated simply as data-points. They ought not be objectified or instrumentalised, for instance, by being treated as slot-filling providers of data. In respecting research participants, we are acknowledging their worth as individual participants and not as inter-changeable pawns in some larger design. That kind of respect begins with noticing — the activity of recognising the particularities of the research participant as someone to be respected.

Recognition — the Perceptual Dimension of Respect

Respect is activated by the combination of noticing, recognition and appreciation. The sense of valuing that is part of respect comes from understanding that respect belongs to the nature of the respect*ed* and not to the nature of the respect*er*. It is by virtue of the characteristics and circumstances of the individual respected — the object of our perceiving — that we value a person, whether in the universal sense or in some particularised sense.

Our perceptions are the response called out by the one to whom we are giving our attention, our recognition of the person we are valuing. Our respect is elicited, even demanded, by people in particular circumstances. There are, then, two bases for my respecting the research participant before me. I respect that person in the way due to all persons. In addition, I may respect him or her, precisely because of the particular circumstances or experiences that have drawn me to invite this individual person into my research environment. I have a research question that can best be addressed by having as participants, persons with particular experiential histories, knowledge or abilities. In our special case, I wish to know more about the experiences of being a refugee early in life. In seeking to recruit a young refugee sample, I recognise that this sample has suffered harm and is susceptible to further harm. I acknowledge that particular condition. They demand my special respect — my protective respect.

When given, then, protective respect is called out and directed towards the one being respected. We do not respect someone, for instance, in the same way that we love them — because of our own feelings and emotions. We respect someone and treat them with respect, because of who they are and who they are in the specific context of their lives.

The Respecter's Attitude and Behaviour

Recognising what is valuable about a particular person also involves recognising the constraints that that value places on our own conduct, and acting in a way that expresses that recognition (Dickert, 2010, p. 313). As the researcher perceives the participants' value and situation, s/he also forms a responsive attitude to that recognition. S/he takes it into her own attitudinal appraisal, and acts upon it.

Taking up the responsiveness dimension, several commentators (including Rawls) ground respect for others in the self-respect of the respecter. They also see a flow-on effect, in enhancing the self-respect of the respected.

In research environments, this responsive, attitudinal component of respect places the moral responsibility of structuring the interaction firmly on the researcher. Respect then becomes a moral imperative, a 'directive' to prompt particular kinds of action (Baier, 1995). When that imperative is put into practice by a respecter, felt respect becomes enacted respect. Due respect becomes actual respect. Then respect is expressed in respectful treatment. What the respectful researcher does in interactions with research participants are varied expressions of respect, for example, in attending to participants' sensitivities to invasion of privacy, or ensuring that they have adequate control over the situation (Dickert, 2010).

There is then a cycle of a self-respecting person perceiving the value of another person, and responding by giving respect that facilitates the receiving person's self-respect. When that cyclical interaction is missing, particularly in the case of young people who have been already denied respect, they are likely to become suspicious of the possibility of further violations. The threat is likely to have adverse effects on their self-respect (Thompson, 1990).

This does not mean that all respect-giving researchers will act in the same way. The call for respect is not a treatise on uniformity. It rather draws attention to the action-provoking nature of the researchers' recognition of the constraints placed upon them as researchers by the state and circumstances of their participants. The giving of respect is a highly particularised activity. It is a matter of how the researcher structures the research environment to maximise the participants' self-respect.

Lack of respect, of course, also is expressed in action. A researcher, for example, may overtly follow ethically regulated procedures, but follow them with a disrespectful attitude. Does that matter? According to Dickert, it certainly does matter, because that disrespect may be communicated to the participant. Such attitudinal disrespect, then, is unlikely to admit the self-respecting cycle into the situation. Instead, it admits the possibility of a self-disrespecting cycle, and within that cycle, further harm.

Dickert lists, for instance, several ways in which a researcher can fail to demonstrate due respect. These include not observing cultural differences, for example, eye contacts between children and adults and hand shaking between the sexes. Lack of respect may also be demonstrated in not providing adequate translations and explanations of plain language statements and consent forms.

By now, the institutionalisation of research ethics should have permeated society well enough for participants to be given the opportunity to understand that their part in research interactions is serious business — that someone has looked carefully at the conditions of their involvement. Those conditions to a large extent revolve around the respect that research*ers* pay to their participants — the research*ees*. Attention to those conditions also helps shape the design of the interaction, in effect, decreasing, and hopefully eliminating the objectification of participants, whereby their personhood and rights are abrogated and they are seen as inter-changeable slot-fillers stripped of the inherent value of personhood.

Implementing Respect in Research Interactions

Giving respect to young refugee research participants is not a matter of applying empty sentiment. There are hard decisions to be made at numbers of points in the process — from the decision to include them in the class of potential participants to the appropriate selection of individuals and groups. Those decisions place considerable respect-driven responsibility on the researcher.

Including Young Refugee Participants

The reasons for including refugee young people in research are directly related to the information they have to give, their ability to provide that authentic information, and their rights to a voice. Alternatively, the reasons for not including refugee young people may stem either from the misguided over-protectionism that we have rejected, or from a researcher's unwillingness to take upon themselves the responsibility of working out how to interact with these young participants with due respect, because of their known vulnerability to harm. Respect needs to be worked out in practice in order to avoid distorting the information gained from including them. Cairns and Dawes (1996), for instance, identified two tendencies that can distort knowledge about displaced young people's lives. One is the tendency to stress the negative, and so to miss vital investigations of their successful adaptations. The other is the tendency to interpret the absence of negative symptoms as resilience, and to miss examining the conditions that make their pathways harder to negotiate. Appropriate application of respect allows the research to avoid such distortions and to make the inclusion of refugee young people in research a positive experience.

The stories they have to tell are far outside the normal experiences of their peers, and are significant for informing the research community and agencies seeking to help optimise their developmental pathways. These stories also have a significance of their own, and need a place of their own in the record of contemporary human life and its global movements. While there is widespread agreement that such information is needed, there still is only a relatively small body of empirical information available, and even less longitudinal information on pathways into community life (McFarlane et al., 2011).

Information collected from other samples cannot serve as bases for understanding the difficulties and triumphs of refugee experiences in young lives. Yet, when searching for empirical evidence, researchers often extrapolate from information gathered from adult samples, or from information gathered from minority and migrant groups whose experiences and stories do not mirror those of refugees (Goodnow, in press). Normative Western young samples are even more problematic as primary sources of insights about young people who have experienced dislocation and trauma.

Acknowledging That There is No Generic Informant

In a similar way, it is not productive to rely on the distinctive circumstances of one refugee group or individual as proxies for the circumstances of other groups or individuals. Just as there is no 'generic child' with information relevant to all children (Cairns & Dawes, 1996; Morrow & Richards, 1996), there is no one piece of empirical information that is applicable to all children of refugee background. No one young person can be treated as 'the generic refugee young person', or as 'the representative refugee young person'. There are particularities in the circumstances and responses of young people who have been displaced, and these defy aggregation. Some, for example, have suffered deliberate torture, some have been dragooned into armies, some have fled natural disasters. Young people who have spent long months in detention are on quite different pathways to recovery than young people whose parents fled by less perilous routes and were given direct entry into their new community (Newman, 2013).

When considering the complex and varied pathways to recovery (VFST, 1996), even information collected about an individual young person at one time will not be perpetually relevant to all the questions we may ask about that young person. Young people are in the process of dynamic developmental change, and the circumstances of their lives are also undergoing dynamic change (Björn & Björn, 2004). The normative changes experienced by all young people are occurring at the same time as the dramatic life changes experienced in transit and resettlement, and these two forms of change may not be in step with each other. Multiple perspectives and multiple data points are needed to track the unique experiences of flight and recovery. 'One hit research' also can be distorting if over-applied or over-interpreted.

Preserving the Right to a Voice

We have emphasised the protective application of respect. A protective approach, however, cannot be allowed to erode the basic human rights of developing persons to have their say. Over-protective sentiments, particularly on the part of review committees, in fact may deny young people a voice. Refugee young people have the right to appropriate opportunities to express themselves. Just as we need them to impart knowledge, they need the opportunity to be heard.

The rights to a voice that are pertinent to research interactions are well covered in the UN Convention on the Rights of the Child (CROC, 1989) by Articles, 10, 12, and 13. They cover, for instance, the rights of children to hold and express their views, and to seek, receive, and impart knowledge appropriate to their age and maturity. The CROC predicated these rights on the ability of children to form and express their views and opinions. Competence and rights, although different, run in parallel, with one informing the other.

Although it is still not universally accepted, there is enough solid evidence to establish that children and young people are able to convey information in the most sensitive of circumstances (e.g., Morrow & Richards, 1996; Parkinson & Cashmore, 2008; Thompson, 1990). Quite young children are able to express their needs, and also to report on both the positive and adverse circumstances that affect their lives.

Young people's expression of their concerns depends largely on the researcher's will and ability to make their authentic contribution possible. That may become difficult to realise in circumstances where other interests are at work. Even with western samples, particularly in the US, it is possible for proposals to give young people a voice to come up against parental wishes and rights. The US is one of only two countries that have not ratified the UN Convention, with lobbying for parents' rights over children a major factor in the unwillingness to sign up (Hicks & Lawrence, 2004). Working out how to give a voice to young people from hierarchically structured cultures may require special insight and diplomacy.

The Researcher's Responsibilities

These considerations about youthful participation in research, once they are approached with the aim of giving due respect, take the discussion away from negativity and prohibitions. They move, instead, towards positive steps for proposing research interactions and positive ways for reviewing those proposals. Considerations of respect do not deny researchers access to children, but give them a framework for making their interactions more positive and productive for all. The discussion then can go forward into how respect affects the ways researchers set up and carry out research interactions with refugee young people that, in Balen et al.'s (2006, p. 42) terms, allows researchers to 'navigate the safest course' towards achieving the 'best interests of the child'.

Deciding what may be in the best interest of a refugee young person involves checking various points of interaction against respect. Researchers committed to giving respect are able to refer their proposed goals and procedures back to the valuing, protective and compensatory criteria, working out how these criteria can be implemented in the features of their specific research interactions. Cicourel (1973) proposed this kind of approach to applying general principles to specific situations. The general, overarching principles (guidelines) are consulted to generate situation-specific working rules that can connect with the specific phenomena in the situation. The working rules then are referred back to the guiding principles to check the appropriateness of both the rules and the principles.

In practical terms, that kind of process means checking whether a proposed outcome or procedure is likely to promote, or alternatively to erode the self-respect of young researchees. Such checks against respect contrast with the kinds of procedures by which researchers may proceed to their own ends by the most convenient procedures (e.g., making assumptions about generic participants or using inappropriate samples). Respect-driven checks also contrast with following institutional requirements with any kind of institutionalised rigidity. In effect, guiding research by respect asks researchers to be on the alert to recognise the vulnerabilities and the potentialities of young refugee participants and to translate respect into action at the various decision points that arise in the life of a research project.

Framing Research Practice by Respect

There is no shortage of accounts of the decision points where respect can and should be guiding decisions for action with children as a general class of research participants (e.g., Morrow & Richards, 1996; NHMRC, 2007; Thompson, 1990). There is, however, a shortage of analyses of the decision points specifically in relation to young refugee participants. If we take seriously Morrow and Richards' (1996) comment that ethical dilemmas arise at various phases in the life of a research project, then we can expect that respect will need to be applied frequently, at several decision points.

Identifying Decision Points

Fisher et al. (2002) made one attempt when they produced a list for the American Psychological Association of points where cultural differences are important when ethnic and minority groups of children are included in research. They specified attending to cultural differences when evaluating risks and benefits, developing and implementing informed consent procedures, securing confidentiality, and consulting potential groups of participants and ethnic communities. Although they were not specifically focusing on refugee participants, their decision points provide at least a starting place when cultural differences are at issue, especially if we do not transpose 'refugee' for 'ethnic'.

With that caveat, the Fisher list is not sufficient for the whole task, because they did not include in their initial list methods, procedures and instruments. Further, some subsequent comments about instruments made by Fisher and colleagues suggest that they had not grappled fully with the issue of aligning methods and measures closely to the lived experiences and interests of potential participant groups. They seemed to be more concerned with standardisation than with tailoring methods to participants; for example they commented that, 'whenever possible, investigators should select instruments that have been standardised on members of the research participants' racial or ethnic group' (p. 1026). 'Whenever possible' seems to be a permissive clause, and standardisation for particular groups (and individuals within those groups) requires deeper examination of how standardised instruments may depend on the kinds of assumptions about generic or representative refugee children that may distort information.

Selecting Methods and Instruments

The psychometric properties of instruments to be used with immigrant and ethnic groups were subjected to closer scrutiny by van de Vijver and Phalet (2004). These authors also commented on the need to tune assessment to the different acculturation experiences of ethnic groups — an issue taken up in relation to refugee groups by Lawrence, Dodds, and Brooker (2010). That kind of 'tuning' involves recognising the different conditions for people coming from other cultures, and also how these conditions may change in different ways (see Björn & Björn, 2004). Some refugee groups, for instance, have better structures in place for providing support for newcomers and their children. The pathways of those supported young people are likely to vary from those who make the transition without cultural support.

It is understandable that researchers will find that particular aspects of their research programs will stand out as decision points for them. Devising respectful procedures for recruiting young refugee participants and for obtaining informed consent are obvious candidates as decision points. The development of culturally-appropriate language and communication styles seem to be other obvious candidates. Less obvious, it seems, for respect-driven monitoring are procedures for reporting back to researchees and their families and recognition of participants' interests in the outcomes and implications of the research.

Developing Suitable Methods and Techniques

Researchers need to be aware of young people's abilities and interests in relation to their circumstances. Young people have natural abilities for telling stories, constructing representative drawings and manipulating objects. Almost all young people are fascinated by technology and computers. Once these and other preferred media are admitted as techniques for data construction, they can provide young people with multiple means of expression. They also provide researchers with multiple vehicles of expressing their respect and of facilitating knowledge construction (Dodds et al., 2010; Zwi, Herzberg, Dossetor, & Field, 2003).

Refugee children are able to report on experiences and activities that assist or impede their wellbeing, when researchers provide them with accessible, culturally appropriate research environments and tasks. As one example, our research group has been using computer-assisted interviews to allow primary school children from varied refugee and nonrefugee backgrounds to report on their skills, wellbeing and their interpretations and feelings about different activities and places in their lives (Dodds et al., 2010; Lawrence et al., 2010). Several of our tasks allow children to express their views without recourse to language. It does not take new arrivals long before they are able to draw on their technical awareness and skills. In addition, we are finding that refugee young people are able to describe some of their feelings by typing into these programs, if the researcher is available to assist with explanations and spelling.

Too often it has been easier to start with materials developed on a known (western) group and then translate those materials for other cultural groups (Goodnow, in press). As an alternative, we are advocating that the process begin with due recognition of refugee young people as a unique group, or more properly, several unique groups from different cultures and places. From that starting place, ideally researchers would work, with respect as a framing device, to develop frameworks, decision criteria and materials with their participants' vulnerability and needs to

the fore. That recognition also involves recognising the susceptibility of refugee young people to the disrespect that erodes self-
respect (Dillon, 2010).

Conclusion

We have argued that the ethical principle of respect is a major
guideline for developing, conducting, and reviewing research in
which researchers interact with refugee young people.
Obviously, respect is not the only ethical guideline to be considered. Similar analyses of justice and benevolence principles may
reveal other areas of research with refugee groups and individuals requiring specific attention. Our aim here was to analyse the
particular significance of respect for a group of young people
who typically have not been treated with due respect in their
lives. In concentrating on respect, we have drawn attention to
the appropriateness of counteracting the susceptibility of
refugee young people to harm and disrespect in research, and of
the possibility of adding to their welfare. We also have addressed
the ethical responsibilities of researchers at the level of one
ethical principle rather than by providing lists of 'do and don't'
rules or even lists of decision points.

We are not advocating a formulaic approach. Rather, we are
proposing the principle of respect as a guide and framing device
for researchers to consult, and also as the basis for their own
perceptions, attitudes and behaviours as they frame and imple-
ment their research interactions. We trust that researchers will
take up the challenge of entering the cycle of self-respecting
research*er* interacting with young research*ees* in ways that
promote their self-respect and the construction of knowledge.

References

Baier, K. (1995). *The rational and the moral order: The social roots of reason and morality.*
Chicago, IL: Open Court.

Balen, R., Blyth, E., Calabretto, H., Fraser, C., Horrocks, C., & Manby, M. (2006).
Involving children in health and social research: 'Human becomings' or 'active
beings'? *Childhood, 13*(1), 29–48.

Bhabha, J., & Crock, M. (2006). *Seeking asylum alone: A comparative study of laws, policy, and practice in Australia, the UK and the US regarding unaccompanied and separated children.* Sydney, Australia: Themis Press.

Björn, G.J., & Björn, A. (2004). Ethical aspects when treating traumatized refugee children and their families. *Nordic Journal of Psychiatry, 58,* 193–198.

Cairns, E., & Dawes, A. (1996). Children: Ethnic and political violence — a commentary. *Child Development, 67*(1), 129–139.

Cicourel, A.V. (1973). *Cognitive sociology: Language and meaning in social interaction.* Harmondsworth, England: Penguin Education.

Correa-Velez, I., Gifford, S.M., & Barnett, A.G. (2010). Longing to belong: Social inclusion and wellbeing among youth with refugee backgrounds in the first three years in Melbourne, Australia. *Social Science & Medicine, 71,* 1399–1408.

Council for International Organizations of Medical Sciences (CIOMS). (1993). International ethical guidelines for biomedical research involving human subjects / prepared by the Council for International Organizations of Medical Sciences (CIOMS) in collaboration with the World Health Organization (WHO). Geneva, Switzerland: Author. Retrieved from http://www.codex. uu.se/texts/international. html#general

Dickert, N.W. (2010). Re-examining respect for human research participants. *Kennedy Institute of Ethics Journal, 19*(4), 311–338.

Dillon, R.S. (1992). Respect and care: Toward moral integration. *Canadian Journal of Philosophy, 22*(1), 105–132.

Dillon, R.S. (2010). Respect for persons, identity, and information technology. *Ethics of Information Technology, 12,* 17–28.

Dodds, A.E., Lawrence, J.A., Karantzas, K., Brooker, A., Lin, Y.H., Champness, V., & Albert, N. (2010). Children of Somali refugees in Australian schools: Self-descriptions of school-related skills and needs. *International Journal of Behavioral Development, 34*(6), 521–528.

Fazel, M., Wheeler, J., & Danesh, J. (2005). Prevalence of serious mental disorder in 7000 refugees resettled in western countries: A systematic review. *Lancet, 365,* 1309–1314.

Fisher, C.B., Hoagwood, K., Boyce, C., Duster, T., Frank, D.A., Grisso, T., … Zayas, L.H. (2002). Research ethics for mental health science involving ethnic minority children and youths. *American Psychologist, 57*(12), 1024–1040.

Goodnow, J.J. (in press). Refugees, asylum seekers, displaced persons: Children in precarious positions. In A. Ben-Arieh, J. Cashmore, G. Goodman, & G. Melton (Eds.), *Handbook of child research.* New York, NY: Sage.

Hicks, A.J., & Lawrence, J.A. (2004). Procedural safeguards for young offenders: Views of legal professionals and adolescents. *The Australian & New Zealand Journal of Criminology, 37*(3), 401–417.

Hurst, S.A. (2008). Vulnerability in research and health care: Describing the elephant in the room? *Bioethics, 22*(4), 191–202.

Kant, I. (1797/1996). Metaphysics of morals. In M. Gregor (Trans. & Ed.), *Practical philosophy.* Cambridge, England: Cambridge University Press.

Lawrence, J.A., & Dodds, A.E. (2010). Three approaches to the disjunction between psychological measurement and psychological persons: Methodological and ethical considerations. *Integrative Psychological & Behavioral Sciences, 44,* 299–309.

Lawrence, J.A., Dodds, A.E., & Brooker, A. (2010). Constructing research knowledge with refugee young people: Using computer-assisted techniques. *International Society for the Study of Behavioural Development Newsletter, November, Serial 58*(2), 26–28.

Levine, C., Faden, R., Grady, C., Eckenwiler, L., & Sugarman, J. (2004). The limitations of 'vulnerability' as a protection for human research participants. *The American Journal of Bioethics, 4*(3), 44–49.

Luster, T., Quin, D., Bates, L., Johnson, D., & Rana, M. (2009). The lost boys of Sudan: Coping with ambiguous loss and separation from parents. *American Journal of Orthopsychiatry, 79*(2), 203–211.

Lustig, S.I., Kia-Keating, M., Knight, W.G., Geltman, P., Ellis, H., Kinzie, D., ... Saxe, G.N. (2004). Review of child and adolescent refugee mental health. *Journal of The American Academy of Child & Adolescent Psychiatry, 43*(1), 24–36.

McFarlane, C.A., Kaplan, I., & Lawrence, J.A. (2011). Psychosocial indicators of wellbeing for resettled refugee children and youth: Conceptual and developmental directions. *Child Indicators Research, 4*(4), 647–677.

Morrow, V., & Richards, M. (1996). The ethics of social research with children: An overview. *Children & Society, 10*, 90–105.

National Health & Medical and Research Council (NHMRC). (2006). *Challenging ethical issues in research on human beings.* Canberra, Australia: Commonwealth of Australia. Retrieved from www.nhmrc.gov.au/publications/

National Health and Medical Research Council, Australian Research Council, & Australian Vice-Chancellors' Committee. (2007). *National Statement on Ethical Conduct in Human Research.* Canberra, Australia: Australian Government.

Newman, L. (2013) Researching immigration detention: Documenting damage and ethical dilemmas. In K. Block, E. Riggs & N. Haslam (Eds.), *Values and vulnerabilities: The ethics of research with refugees and asylum seekers.* Brisbane, Australia: Australian Academic Press.

Parkinson, P., & Cashmore, J. (2008). *The voice of a child in family law disputes.* Oxford, England: Oxford University Press.

Rawls, J. (1971). *A theory of justice.* Cambridge, MA: Harvard University Press.

Thompson, R.A. (1990). Vulnerability in research: A developmental perspective on research risk. *Child Development, 61*, 1–16.

United Nations. (1989). *Convention on the Rights of the Child.* Geneva, Switzerland: Author.

United Nations High Commission for Refugees. (1994). *Guidelines on protection and care.* Geneva, Switzerland: Author.

United States National Institute of Health. (1979). The Belmont Report: Ethical principles and guidelines for the protection of human subjects in research. Retrieved from http://ohsr.od. nih.gov/guidelines/belmont.html

Van de Vijver, F.J. R., & Phalet, K. (2004). Assessment in multicultural groups. *Applied Psychology: An International Review, 53*(2), 215–236.

Victorian Foundation for Survivors of Torture (VFST). (1996). *Guide to working with young people who are refugees.* Melbourne, Australia: Author.

Williams, R. (2007). The psychosocial consequences for children of mass violence, terrorism and disasters. *International Review of Psychiatry, 19*(3), 263–277.

Zwi, K.J., Herzberg, B., Dossetor, D., & Field, J. (2003). A child in detention: Dilemmas faced by health professionals. *The Medical Journal of Australia, 179*(6), 319–322.

CHAPTER

7

Ethical Approaches in Research With Refugees and Asylum Seekers Using Participatory Action Research

Hariz Halilovich

Social research has traditionally been focused on 'outsiders': problematic, 'deviant', issue-generating, disadvantaged and marginalised groups. Even though much of the 'labelling language' has changed, these social groups — still perceived as deviating from what is considered normal, ordinary, mainstream and 'us' — continue to be disproportionately put under the gaze of social researchers in their quest to uncover social abnormalities and issues. Affected by a plethora of 'abnormalities' — including displacement, dispossession, homelessness, poverty, unemployment, violence and 'illegal' migration — refugees have had a prominent role among groups deviating from what is considered socially 'normal' and 'ordinary'. Hence, it is not surprising that refugees often end up 'under the spotlight' in various research projects which explore different aspects of 'refugeeness', that is 'otherness'.

In addition to international organisations such as UNHCR and IOM, research into refugees is regularly commissioned and financially supported by governments hosting refugees on a temporary or permanent basis, as well as by government agencies desiring to keep refugees away from their nation-state borders. The aim of much 'commissioned' research is to identify and categorise displaced groups and 'refugee issues' in order to provide policy recommendations about how most efficiently to deal with the 'problems' 'generated' by refugees. In the 'age of migration', as Castles and Miller (2003) termed it, the mobility of refugees and asylum seekers has increasingly been perceived as a threat to the sovereignty and national homogeneity of nation states. However, as Huyssen concludes, 'in an era of 'ethnic cleansing' and refugee crises, mass migrations and global mobility for ever more people, the experience of displacement and relocation, migration and diaspora seems no longer the exception, but the rule' (2003, p. 25). In the political arena and populist media in many developed countries, including Australia,[1] rather than recognising refugees as individuals needing protection under enshrined UN conventions, it has been a common practice to accuse refugees of all sorts of social ills and wrongs, from violating borders to lacking integration potential, being welfare cheats, queue jumpers, and even likely terrorists (Bolt, 2009; Dhanji, 2009).

In this chapter, in addition to pointing to some subtle (and not so subtle) prejudices about refugees and asylum seekers, I argue for a stronger interconnectedness between methodology and ethics in refugee research, as 'how we do research?' and 'why we bother doing it?' are the quintessential questions that cannot, or should not, be separated when researching people fleeing persecution and in need of protection. While focusing on very specific, often local and regional contexts, refugee research ultimately tackles much broader questions of the human condition in relation to politically motivated violence, persecution of minorities, forced displacement and the violation of fundamental human rights. Thus, researching these pertinent contemporary issues under the umbrella of refugee research requires more than a good grasp of relevant theories and research techniques, ultimately demanding researchers to actively engage in advancing human rights and advocate for the dignity and safety of their participants. As I describe in this chapter, one way to align research methodology with ethics and accomplish research objectives, while maintaining professional integrity as a researcher can be to adopt participatory action research as an approach to both researching and teaching refugee issues.

Ethics and Politics of Refugee Research

Refugees and asylum seekers, 'by definition', are highly vulnerable people whose lives and freedoms are threatened, while their 'well-founded fear' relates to threats of death, torture, starvation, rape, robbery and other forms of cruel, inhuman or degrading treatment.[2] However, many nonrefugees, including those who write about refugees, often fail to recognise that 'being a refugee' does not equate to some distinct individual or collective identity; rather, it defines a temporary — and more often than not a prolonged — state in which ordinary people find themselves, when going through extraordinary ordeals as a result of social and political upheaval in their homelands. Numerous examples from modern history and the times we live in only confirm that anyone could become subject to persecution and be turned into a refugee. Yet, there is still a widespread perception in 'host countries' that refugees are a homogenous collective that somehow has to do more with 'them' than with 'us'. Hence the word 'refugee' usually has negative connotations, disregarding the individual aspects of refugee experiences and reducing the identity of diverse groups of people to only one of their life episodes — that of fleeing persecution and leaving their homelands (Halilovich, 2006, p. 60).

As people who have gone through dramatic flights and traumatic experiences, refugees continue to attract diverse reactions in countries where they seek protection. These reactions range from being blamed for their own misery to being patronised and perceived as powerless and exotic victims. Sometimes researchers writing about the sufferings of refugees may contribute to such perceptions, even though, as Bakewell points out, the origins of refugee studies 'arose from a concern about highlighting their particular situations, defending their rights and bringing them into the sight of international policy action to improve their situation' (2008, p. 440). While focusing on the violations of the human rights of refugees, other aspects of refugee experiences often get overlooked. As Uehling (1998, p. 124) put it: 'if we become fixed on [the] notion of violation, we will fail to recognize the ways in which refugees are actively building their world'. In other words, as important as it is to point to the traumatic aspects of refugee experiences, it is also critical to recognise the resilience of people coming out of such experiences.

While 'trauma' has become a dominant keyword in refugee research, I consciously avoid using the concept of 'trauma' when describing and referring to refugee experiences, memories and narratives. In my view — based on both my research experience with refugees and my professional roles as a former counsellor and mental health worker working with refugees and asylum seekers in Australia and Germany — the overuse of the term trauma has led to the medicalisation and pathologising of human suffering, and in particular of the memories and experiences of refugees and survivors of violence (Lambert, Haasen, & Halilovich, 1998). As Summerfield argues, there are prevalent assumptions today in the west 'that the experience of war routinely generates not just suffering or misery but 'posttraumatic stress', a pathological condition affecting large numbers of those exposed and who need attention for this' (2004, p. 239). Rather than looking for signs of trauma as a disabling condition, researchers should be encouraged to look for a diversity of experiences within the researched refugee groups.

In order to uncover the rich diversity within each refugee population, as well as to reach people affected by violence and forced displacement who may not necessarily fit the official category of 'refugee', researchers are sometimes required to go beyond official categories that regulate the status of the displaced (Bakewell, 2008; DeWind, 2007; Martin, 2000). Such groups of people — referred to as IDPs, asylum seekers, illegal immigrants, unlawful noncitizens, trafficked persons, detainees, and so on — often remain in 'refugee-like' situations for years, without being formally recognised as refugees by the UNHCR or 'host' governments. Thus, when drawing their own conclusions about human suffering caused by forced displacement, researchers may be required to bypass, or take with reservations, the official bureaucracies and their classifications of people affected by violence and displacement. As Birman warns, 'ethical issues are also involved in refugee admissions policies that may cause great suffering for those whose asylum claims may be denied, forcing them to return to their native country' (2006, p. 155).

Different social contexts and government policies impact on how we conduct research into the issues of refugee and asylum seekers, 'often undertaken in politically complex, difficult and sometimes dangerous settings and with participants who may be traumatized and vulnerable' (Mackenzie, McDowell, & Pittaway, 2007, p. 299). Notwithstanding this fact, Cushman (2004, p. 7) argues that scholars are bound by two main ethical obligations: first, to avoid producing work that legitimises or rationalises the accounts of the perpetrators of mass violence; and, second, to avoid producing accounts that deny the phenomenological realities of social suffering. These ethical imperatives imply that refugee research can never be apolitical or 'objectively neutral'. Despite this, even when researching crimes against humanity and genocide, some researchers believe that an objective, apolitical neutrality is achievable. In some cases, 'blinded by the myths of objectivity and the mask of scientific methodology, professionals are able to distance themselves, in the name of scientific rigor, from emotional confrontation with mass death' (Hirsch, 1995, p. 85). The researchers who do manage to avoid the 'trap of scientism' — as Hirsch (1995) put it — in most instances may not have a 'pre-emptive' political agenda but rather become 'circumstantial activists' and 'engaged observers' in the course of their research (Marcus, 1998). The most common reason for their action is simply the fact that they 'cannot escape physically, ethically and emotionally the suffering and the brutality of their research subject and the historical epoch they live in' (Bourgois, 2006, p. xii).

Researching communities after systematic violence — the result and intent of which is forced displacement — in itself provides sufficient moral justification for social researchers to take a more pro-active role in speaking along with, not on behalf of, those they research. Such an approach does not compromise the validity of their research. On the contrary — as Sanford (2006, p. 14) argues — 'activist scholarship reminds us that all research is inherently political, even, and perhaps especially, that scholarship presented under the guise of 'objectivity', which is really no more than a veiled defence of the status quo'. Keeping the status quo could simply translate into passive support of institutions and individuals responsible for human rights abuses inflicted upon those we research and write about. In order to prevent becoming indifferent observers or passive bystanders, Turton suggests that researchers involved in refugee research need to include the alleviation of human suffering as an 'explicit objective of their research' and ultimately aim to influence the behaviour and thinking of policymakers and practitioners, so that their interventions are more likely to improve than worsen the situation of refugees and displaced people (Turton, 1996, p.96). However, this does not mean that scientific rigour is compromised in refugee research. As Jacobsen and Landau (2003) argue, scientific rigour in refugee research is an important ethical responsibility of researchers, who need to produce credible data that can contribute to public policy debates and be used to influence policies affecting refugees. When interpreting research findings and writing about people affected by violence, Hernandez Castillo (2006) points to the 'double challenge' the researchers face: the need to develop theoretical explanations and frameworks without losing the meaning of the experience of violence for those affected.

While it is critical not to treat refugees as powerless victims, it is also important to recognise the power relations in the contexts in which the research takes place. Among others, research contexts may be a refugee camp, asylum seekers' centre, temporary refugee shelter, detention centre or immigration processing centre. In many of these situations, refugees are deprived of most of what could be considered 'a normal life'. In contrast to the stigma, trauma, well-founded fear of persecution, cultural and language barriers and all the legal limitations imposed on refugees by various parties, researchers — with their institutional affiliations, academic influence, social position, freedom of movement and professional networks — can be perceived by refugees as powerful agents able to change their situation. Krulfeld (1998) argues that researchers must be mindful of these 'structural inequalities' and ensure that research does not lead to the further disempowerment of refugees. She suggests that this ethical concern can be resolved by designing and utilising a 'research approach that incorporates members of the studied community as full co-partners in the research' (Krulfeld, 1998, p. 26). Similarly, Pittaway et al. (2010, pp. 241–242) argue that 'ethics should be extended to promoting the interests and well-being of extremely vulnerable research subjects, in ways that make sense for the research subjects, as well as for researchers and their academic institutions and professional bodies'. Referring to a 'dual imperative', Jacobsen and Landau (2003, p. 1) point out that refugee research needs to satisfy the demands of the academy as well as ensure that knowledge generated is used to protect refugees, influence governments, and improve the ways institutions do their work with refugees.

While it is desired that any research into refugees would directly or indirectly benefit the refugees in question, researchers need to be candid about the limits of their sphere of influence and their power to change the refugees' situation. Developing and sustaining a trusting, mutually respectful and reciprocal relationship between the researcher and the researched is critical. Kirsch, an anthropologist, emphasises the importance of reciprocity as the underlining practice of anthropology, arguing that the ethnographers' 'activism is the logical extension of the commitment to reciprocity' (2002, p. 178).

Cultural sensitivity is another ethical concern, especially when the researcher comes from a different cultural background than that of the refugees, as is most often the case. Cultural sensitivity in a research context is much more than a question of political correctness or humble politeness and, as Birman insists, 'researchers need to tailor ethical guidelines to the ways in which ethical issues are viewed by the culture of the community being studied' (2006, p. 164). This relates to many practical as well as ontological questions that different cultures may deal with differently. For instance, the researcher may need to find culturally acceptable ways when obtaining informed consent from their participants as reading and signing a document may not be appropriate for a variety of reasons, including suspicion of signing forms and lack of literacy (Pittaway et al., 2010). Maintaining confidentiality is another important ethical imperative, which also needs to fit into the cultural norms of those being studied as well as to meet the researchers' institutional ethics requirements. As Birman concludes, when conducting research in a cross-cultural context, the researcher is expected to 'act ethically according to the norms of both cultures involved' (2006, p. 164).

To bridge both cultures, especially those involving linguistic differences, researchers often rely on interpreters and translators, the 'invisible actors' in the research process. While it is important, wherever possible, to ensure their professional integrity and legally binding professional code of practice, it is often the case that language assistants come from the same refugee communities and may lack professional training and accreditation as interpreters. Rather than an ethical barrier, interpreters with insider status may indeed provide invaluable input into the research, contributing much more than mere language aid by interpreting the meanings of different cultural practices and codes, and by adding their own voice to the research. The assistance of interpreters can also be highly valuable in the analysis of research data, as their knowledge can help us 'uncover the richness embedded in the data and facilitate multiple ways of knowing' (Pui-Hing Wong & Kwong-Lai Poon, 2010, p. 151). Thus, the interpreters' involvement in research should never be seen as 'just a technical job'; it is highly appropriate — and ethical — to recognise their important role in the research process by acknowledging them as research assistants or research collaborators. However, these relationships can also be very complex in local research contexts; thus it is important for researchers to be able to recognise and resolve any ethical and methodological issues that may be associated with the use of local interpreters and assistants (Jacobsen & Landau, 2003).

Power imbalance and structural inequalities are also present in the research context when the principal researcher speaks the same language and may share the same cultural background as the participants. In such a scenario, the researcher embodies a dual insider–outsider role by positioning himself with respect to his participants as both a cultural insider and a professional outsider 'doing his academic job' (Halilovich, 2011a). Being a cultural insider does not automatically mean an advantage for the researcher, as lack of 'cultural filters' may expose the researcher to additional aspects of the suffering of his respondents. In addition, the researcher may be put under pressure by the expectation of the participants. Nonetheless, I cannot but agree with Voloder (2008), who argues that by utilising self as a resource and adding elements of autoethnography, cultural insiders can enrich refugee research by combining both emic and etic perspectives. Similarly, in her book *Reflexive Ethnography*, Davies argues that all researchers are to some degree connected to, or part of, the object of their research and that 'not only the personal history of ethnographers but also the disciplinary and broader sociocultural circumstances under which they work have a profound effect on which topic and peoples are selected for study' (2008, p. 5).

All the ethical concerns and complexities raised here — and the list is far from being exhaustive — confirm the interrelatedness between ethical and methodological aspects of refugee research.

Methods and Methodologies in Refugee Research

The complexities relating to refugee research — involving many specific and broader factors — require from researchers both flexibility to respond to the particularities of the situations of their participants and creativity to develop 'customised' methods and methodologies, rather than relying on standardised research techniques. The sheer magnitude of the forced displacement of millions of men, women and children worldwide renders any standardised approach and generalisation problematic and unrepresentative. While over the years I have worked with and studied refugee communities from Europe, Africa and Asia, in this chapter, rather than lumping these different groups together, I limit my analysis and descriptions to displaced people from Bosnia-Herzegovina[3] with whom I have worked most extensively — both with IDPs and returnees within Bosnia and refugees overseas: in Austria, Sweden, Australia and the US. While not subscribing to the view that researchers need to come from the same or similar cultural background in order to understand their subjects (van de Port, 1999), being a 'cultural insider' has definitely been an advantage in understanding the issues, gaining access to prospective participants and establishing trusting relationships with them. Being seen and accepted as an insider has provided access to information that might have been off limits to outside researchers (Hermann, 2001).

Even within this 'single' displaced group, representing a small cross-section of some 2.2 million Bosnians who have been affected by forced displacement, there is a myriad of phenomenological realities as people have been affected by forced displacement and violence in many different ways and on many different levels: individual, family, communal and societal. Consequently, I have made a deliberate decision to go beyond — and below — demographic, ethnic and statistical categories in order to unveil the deeper understandings of the reality of displacement as experienced by those affected. In doing this, I have tailored my methodological approach to fit both the context and the desired 'research impact' for each 'subgroup' I researched. This involved combining and supplementing conventional ethnography with multisited and digital ethnography and treating my research participants as collaborators in the research projects — and thus effectively practising participatory action research.

As participatory action research is not a single research method — like focus groups, interviews or surveys, for instance — but rather a complex methodology and 'an alternative philosophy of social research' (Kemmis & McTaggart 2000, p. 568), this research approach is open to interpretation and diverse applications in various research areas and contexts. What is commonly shared between the different understandings and applications of participatory action research, however, is the focus on the participants' inclusion in the research process as both research subjects and research collaborators. As such, participatory action research is especially applicable to researching different communities when conducting ethnographic fieldwork.

Another important aspect of participatory action research is its focus on the empowerment of participants through the research process and outcomes. In other words, 'participatory action research aims to examine political structures that disempower marginalised, deprived and oppressed people and to find ways in which these structures can be changed' (Liamputtong & Ezzy, 2005). Thus, it is not surprising that a number of researchers have recognised the applicability of participatory action research as an effective methodology in refugee research (Doná, 2007; Johannsen, 2001; O'Neill, Woods, & Webster, 2005; Pittaway et al., 2010; van der Velde, 2009). While participatory action research is not exclusively based on qualitative research methods, anthropologists and other qualitative researchers favouring ethnographic research have been at the forefront of this methodology, incorporating it in other methodological para-digms such as critical ethnography and applied anthropology.

As an anthropologist researching the effects of forced dis-placement on local communities, I have adopted — and adapted — participatory action research as an integral part of my multisited ethnography involving refugees, IDPs and 'returnees'. At times, my ethnography moves into the domain of 'critical ethnography', defined as 'conventional ethnography with a political purpose' (Thomas, 1993, as cited in Madison, 2005, p. 1). At times my critical ethnography moves into applied anthropology — that is, 'use of anthropological knowledge and skill in solving practical problems in the field' (van Willigen, 2002, p. ix). Combining critical ethnography and applied anthropology with participatory action research in the field, above all means developing and sustaining collaboration with members of the researched community aimed at a positive transformation of the community in question. Such collabora-tion — in which academic research turns into social action — often happens spontaneously rather than pre-emptively and is a result of a deep and mostly long-term engagement between the researcher and the researched (Stull & Schensul, 1987).

Social action in refugee research using ethnography can also be seen in its documentary role, collecting and cataloguing yet untold stories that deserve to be written down, passed on and subjected to scholarly exploration. By including such stories in our research findings, presentations and publications, we are bringing them — and not just symbolically — from the margins to the centre, from the private into the public domain. By practising participatory action research, rather than appropriating the right to speak on the participants' behalf, researchers become co-facilitators of a social change directly or indirectly leading to the empowerment of the participants/collaborators. There are many possible ways to do this, and, as stated earlier, local circumstances and social contexts have a decisive role in how and if participatory action research will be conducted. When researching refugees, like any other group, any potential risks the research may involve must be carefully assessed and weighed against prospective benefits. Hence, in addition to aiming for a positive social change leading to the empowerment of the displaced, ethnographers involved in participatory action research need to negotiate all the complexities the fieldwork involves by responding to challenges creatively and ethically (Smith, 2009).

'Aussie' Bosnians from Germany

Before embarking on fieldwork to study the realities of forced displacement of Bosnians in other countries, I started my research with Bosnian refugees in Melbourne and Adelaide. The first group of refugees whom I contacted were young Bosnian teenagers, who lost members of their families during the war (Halilovich, 2006). After fleeing Bosnia at the beginning or during the war, they spent up to 10 years in Germany, and then migrated to Australia in the late 1990s and early 2000. Most of them lived with their mothers — who became war widows — and siblings of a similar age in traditional migrant suburbs in the two cities. I started my research with individual interviews with the teenagers, exploring their refugee experiences. I visited them at their new homes and their new schools. One of my first research findings was that these Bosnian youth were very 'German', that is they were profoundly attached to the life they had left behind in Germany. Most of them were too young to remember Bosnia, but their memories of Germany — where they went to school and spent their formative years — were vivid and fresh. Their 'first language' was German rather than Bosnian and their *Heimweh* (longing/homesickness) for Germany was more prominent than for their first homeland Bosnia. I also found that they felt quite isolated and alienated within both the wider Bosnian refugee community and Australian society at large. Due to their 'Germanness', they lacked cultural connections and shared experiences with their Bosnian peers who came to Australia directly from Bosnia or other countries. In most cases they did not know many of their peers who came from Germany, as back in Germany they lived in different places and large cities like Berlin, Munich or Hamburg, while here, in Melbourne and Adelaide, they were dispersed across different suburbs. Due to the 'culture shock' caused by yet another displacement, they spent much of their time at home, chatting with and emailing their friends back in Germany, indulging nostalgically in their 'old' photo albums and music, speaking German with their siblings and generally feeling quite down. Having identified their social isolation and feelings of double alienation — towards both their Australian and Bosnian peers — as the most pressing issues affecting them on a daily basis, I decided to modify my research methods and complement individual interviews with focus groups, where I would bring all the participants together to talk about common issues and most importantly enable them to meet other 'Aussie Bosnians from Germany'. They all agreed that this might be a good practical idea and together we devised the main themes and activities to be discussed. The focus groups turned into popular social gatherings that expanded beyond formal discussion times. They achieved all the desired outcomes: they addressed the social isolation of young Bosnian German-speaking refugees as they gained an avenue where they could speak German, discuss their distinct experiences and make new friends. They were also able to use these contacts as 'social capital' by learning from each other how to make an advantage out of their proficiency in German, choosing German as a Victorian Certificate of Education subject in high school and thus improving their results, which increased their chances of getting into a university course of their choice. A number of them continued studying German and years later many were able to benefit from their multilingualism in professional careers. In this case, by turning conventional research into participatory action research, together with my participants, I was able to facilitate a positive change with a long-lasting impact in the lives of the participants.

Bosnian Women's Group

My second research challenge, where I felt compelled to modify the research design and apply elements of participatory action research, involved researching the effects of forced displacement on Bosnian refugee women who settled in Melbourne. In addition to having the largest concentration of Bosnian migrants in Australia, Melbourne also has the largest number of Bosnian female-headed families. In most instances, the female-headed families are the result of war and the loss of husbands, although a number of families were fractured by divorce after migration. This 'second phase' of my research into Bosnian refugees was a logical extension of my earlier research project involving Bosnian adolescents. As I visited participants in their homes, I met other members of their families. I was constantly reminded of the absence of fathers and husbands from families. Their absence was memorialised in the form of photographic images, regularly enshrined on the walls and in cabinets in living rooms — wedding photos, school photos, and photos of other moments capturing happier times when families were complete. The photos not only tell stories about who the missing people once were, but also remind the women survivors of their own past lives as wives, daughters and family and community members. While mostly men perished in the war, what often gets overlooked is that these men were attached to women as their husbands, fathers, brothers, and sons. Despite these obvious facts, as McPherson et al. (2010) point out, much of the women's suffering and experiences of violence remain invisible.

Loss, grief, missing relatives, displacement, social isolation, single parenthood, financial hardship, psychological health and struggle to reconstruct fragmented families have all been a part of the experiences of the women with whom I conducted my research (Halilovich, 2011b). While this set of issues represented 'rich research data', more importantly it was — and continues to be — an integral part of the lives of my research participants. In order to address some of these issues, I referred the women to organisations such as Australian Red Cross (tracing services) and migrant resource centres (for a range of migration-related issues), and acted as a mediator between them and the 'service providers'. As many of the issues affected many women in a very similar way, together with settlement and health services in Melbourne's western suburbs, we looked into the ways these issues could be addressed in a comprehensive and sustained way. This is how the Bosnian Women's Group (BWG) in Melbourne was established. The group consisted of some fifty Bosnian women, and was open not only to war widows but also to other Bosnian refugee women. With my active support and advocacy, group meetings and activities were facilitated and organised by social workers, community nurses and counsellors working for a settlement service or community health organisation in the area. The BWG was ethnically mixed, but the women rejected being head-counted as Bosniaks, Croats or Serbs;[4] they preferred to identify themselves by their common, inclusive and ethnically neutral denominator 'Bosnian'. In fact, they decided to call their group *Ostanimo zajedno* ('Let's stay together'), referring to their pro-multicultural leanings. The most noticeable diversity in the group was not ethnicity but age difference, as it included women from their mid-twenties to late seventies. Some of them had lost multiple family members across two or three generations.

In addition to providing 'parenting advice', the group addressed some common psychosocial and settlement issues, including women's physical and mental health. The program of the BWG included educational, recreational and social activities. Many meetings turned into grieving sessions, but there were also occasions when all the women 'laughed until they cried', as one of the participants put it. For many of them it was the only time they went together to the city, museums, galleries, and even to a women's circus and a beauty salon for make-up sessions. They acknowledged that, in the last two decades, these had been the rare occasions when they were encouraged to have fun together. They rediscovered that, in addition to having a common identity as 'war widows', 'single mothers' and refugees, they shared with each other the fact that they were women migrants in a completely new cultural environment. They were very keen to discover this new environment and possibly reinvent themselves as 'migrants'. By facilitating the establishment of this group, one research outcome was to raise awareness of the issues of Bosnian war widows, making them visible to the health and community services, who then responded to their needs by developing specialised programs with them and for them. Such a 'customised' approach to participatory action research into different refugee subgroups is critical because — as Nolin (2006, p. 32) argues — 'until recently, women were statistically invisible in migration data and ignored in policy, research and action as if they were less affected by migration experiences than men'.

Researching Displacement in Places of Pain

As a part of my doctoral research exploring forced displacement, popular memory and identity in war-torn communities, I went on to conduct research among IDPs and returnees back in Bosnia and with Bosnian refugees who settled in Austria,

Sweden and the US, the western countries with the largest number of Bosnian refugees.

Once in the field, there was no easy way out of the 'ethnographer-activist' role, nor was I looking for an easy escape. Instead, I learned that doing multisited ethnography of forced displacement inevitably leads into researching and dealing with the harsh realities of causes and consequences. Forced displacement executed through the policy of 'ethnic cleansing' in Bosnia and Herzegovina between 1992 and 1995 was carried out through the systematic violation of human rights, the complete disregard for the lives and dignity of others, and war crimes that culminated in the 1995 Srebrenica genocide (Hoare, 2003). Therefore, any 'average Bosnian story' of displacement has to include dispossession, personal loss, dramatic flights and homelessness. For me, these stories represent some of the most profound and cathartic experiences I have had — as a researcher and a person.

I followed my participants' stories literally across the globe and, in some cases, I went back with my 'storytellers' to their destroyed homes and places that are no more. In this way, I was able to 'visualise' their stories by linking them to the material evidence of their past lives. I was invited to their wedding celebrations, the first birthdays of their children, and the mass graves and funerals of their loved ones who perished in the war.

On a number of separate occasions in the course of my research, I was presented with testimonies of horrific war crimes and information about war criminals who continue to benefit from their deeds. Some of these testimonies were first-hand witness accounts, while other stories were recollections of narratives told and remembered by others. While tempted to use the full names of alleged war criminals as reported by my respondents, I opted for their initials. However, I made contact with war crime investigators and passed on information about crimes I was told about and for which I saw evidence. Many of my respondents insisted on my keeping their original names and their identities in my publications. They were worried if they were to 'hide behind fake names' their stories would not be believed. Participating in the research provided them with an opportunity to get their stories 'off their chests', to have them told to and recorded by someone who cared and showed sincere interest in them. Thus my publications need to be much more than a collection of interesting and often moving stories put in a theoretical framework and analytically dissected. They are above all a reminder, a written memorial to all those who perished and an affirmation of those who survived but whose stories would not have been otherwise heard and remembered (Halilovich, 2011a).

This might alarm 'traditionally-oriented' social researchers, for whom scholars have been expected to convey their research findings in the text as rational, academic, task-oriented, scientific and apolitical — with the personal and literary considered soft, lacking in rigour, too subjective, even emotional and feminine (Nelson, 2011). But, as Bruner (1993) argues, writing is inherently a political act. 'Those who claim', Bruner writes, 'that what is literary is not political or that humanistic interpretative anthropology does not deal with political issues are rather dead wrong' (1993, p. 6). I have not tried to disguise the fact that the topic of my research, the issues explored, the research findings and their broader social impacts are highly political. It would have been impossible, as well as unethical, to explore issues of discrimination, marginalisation, war crimes and genocide without making these political issues the subject of social action. As Sanford (2006, p. 31) put it, 'issues of authority and subjectivity matter to all who work in the field trying to contextualise and sometimes categorise the meaning of surviving genocide and other crimes against humanity'.

Confronted with the magnitude of the loss of human lives and the continuing institutional discrimination against a handful of 'returnees' and those visiting or contemplating joining them back in their destroyed villages and towns years after they fled, my advocacy and activism has been an 'emergency response' prompted by 'an ethical responsibility to address processes of unfairness and injustice' (Madison 2005, p.5). In addition to public speaking, presenting papers at international conferences and seminars, speaking on radio and TV, participating in documentaries, publishing a number of articles and interviews — not only in academic journals but in widely read newspapers, magazines and online portals within and outside Bosnia-Herzegovina — I have also developed and collaborated on implementing innovative education programs on refugee issues, forced displacement and reconciliation. In collaboration with local communities in Bosnia and colleagues in Australia, Austria and the US, I have led international study tours involving a fieldwork-based educational program for undergraduate and postgraduate students. The main objective of this combination of participatory action research and an experiential learning approach to teaching has been to enable students and young researchers to explore and learn firsthand about the effects of forced displacement on local communities by directly engaging with members of such communities, as well as to identify ways in which these devastated communities could be supported (Adams, 2006; Adams, 2008; Halilovich, 2008).

Conclusion

In this chapter I have advocated a case for ethical research of the displaced that goes beyond bureaucratic institutional requirements and the rigidity of discipline-based methodologies. I have argued that methodological approaches need to reflect ethical imperatives when confronted with the human suffering of those we research — as researchers should never allow themselves to become mere 'neutral' and 'objective' observers, that is bystanders, in the face of human suffering. They are ethically obliged — within their power, resources and abilities — to work at actively protecting and advancing the human rights and dignity of their informants. Indeed, as Smyth (2001, pp. 8–9) points out, in such circumstances, 'it may be impossible to remain rigidly within the research role, and not cross the line into intervention'. Crossing that line, and engaging with their participants in action-oriented research, also implies that the ethical imperative *primum non nocere*[5] is not sufficient when researching refugee communities subjected to various human rights abuses, ranging from 'banal' institutional discrimination to their physical annihilation. It is important to reiterate these key ethical imperatives of research undertaken in a refugee context as the plight of refugees worldwide still continues to be exploited for the benefits of researchers only, while the researched often remain left and forgotten in their predicament (Fritz, 2000). Unlike the researchers who can always pack their stuff, complete the project and go home, or wherever they like, and then turn their research data into publications and the advancement of their professional careers, millions of uprooted and destitute people continue to be unwanted and in many cases stripped of everything but their bare humanity — their dignity remaining their last safe refuge. Defending this last refuge of fellow humans is the threshold below which no researcher should ever be willing to go.

Notes

1. At the time of writing this chapter, Australia is marking 10 years since the infamous 'Tampa crisis', the incident that divided Australian society and resulted in an international controversy between Norway and Australia. In August 2001, the Norwegian ship 'MV Tampa' saved 438 Afghan asylum seekers from a sinking vessel on the way to Australia. The Australian Government refused to allow the Norwegian ship to enter Australian waters, directing the refugees to the island-state of Nauru in the Pacific, a policy that became known as the 'Pacific Solution'. Ten years later many things have changed in Australia, including the conservative Howard-led government being replaced by a Labor government. However, when it comes to the government's attitude towards refugees hardly anything changed. When elected in 2007, the Labor government abolished the 'Pacific Solution' only to introduce another version of the same policy in 2011, the so called 'Malaysian Solution', which involves sending asylum seekers arriving in Australia to Malaysia.
2. Convention Relating to the Status of Refugees (http://untreaty.un.org/cod/avl/ha /prsr/prsr.html).

3. I use interchangeably the full official name of the country Bosnia-Herzegovina and its shorter and widely used name Bosnia.

4. Bosniaks (or Bosnian Muslim), Bosnian Serbs and Bosnian Croats are the constitutive ethnic groups of Bosnia-Herzegovina.

5. Latin phrase meaning: 'First, do no harm', or 'Above all, do no harm'.

References

Adams, R. (2006). Srebrenica: Learning from Australian–Bosnian students. *Local-Global: Identity, Security, Community, 2,* 142–153.

Adams, R. (2008). Capacity–building in Bosnia-Herzegovina: The challenge for universities. *Cesaa Review, 35,* 45–56.

Bakewell, O. (2008). Research beyond the categories: The importance of policy irrelevant research into forced migration. *Journal of Refugee Studies, 21*(4), 432–453.

Birman, D. (2006). Ethical issues in research with immigrants and refugees. In Joseph E. Trimble & Celia B. Fisher (Eds.), *The handbook of ethical research with ethnocultural populations and communities* (pp.155–178). Thousand Oaks, CA: Sage.

Bolt, A. (2009). Andrew Bolt Blog: Terror raids. *Herald Sun.* Retrieved from http://blogs. news.com.au/heraldsun/andrewbolt/index.php/heraldsun/comments/terror_raids/

Bourgois, P. (2006). Anthropology in the global state of emergency. In V. Sanford & A. Angel-Ajani (Eds.), *Engaged observer: Anthropology, advocacy and activism* (pp. ix–xii). New Brunswick, Canada: Rutgers University Press.

Bruner, E.M. (1993). Introduction: The ethnographic self and the personal self. In P. Benson (Ed.), *Anthropology and literature* (pp. 1–26). Urbana & Chicago: University of Illinois Press.

Castles, S. & Miller, J.M. (2003). *The age of migration: International population movements in the modern world* (3rd ed.). New York, NY: Guilford Press.

Cushman, T. (2004). Anthropology and genocide in the Balkans. *Anthropological Theory, 4*(1), 5–28.

Davies, C.A. (2008). *Reflexive ethnography: A guide to researching selves and others.* London, England: Routledge.

DeWind, J. (2007). Response to Hathaway. *Journal of Refugee Studies, 20*(3), 381–85.

Dhanji, S. (2009). Welcome or unwelcome? Integration issues and the resettlement of former refugees from the Horn of Africa and Sudan in metropolitan Melbourne. *Australasian Review of African Studies, 30*(2), 152–178.

Doná, G. (2007). The microphysics of participation in refugee research. *Journal of Refugee Studies, 20*(2), 210–229.

Fritz, M. (2000). *Lost on earth: Nomads of the New World.* New York, NY: Routledge.

Halilovich, H. (2011a). Beyond the sadness: Memories and homecomings among survivors of 'ethnic cleansing' in a Bosnian village. *Memory Studies Journal, 4*(1), 42–52.

Halilovich, H. (2011b). (Per)forming 'trans-local' homes: Bosnian diaspora in Australia. In M. Valenta & S. Ramet (Eds.), *Bosnian diaspora: Integration in transnational communities* (pp. 63–82). Farnham, England: Ashgate.

Halilovich, H. (2008). Ethics, human rights and action research: Doing and teaching ethnography in post-genocide communities in Bosnia–Herzegovina. *Narodna Umjetnost Croatian Journal of Ethnology and Folklore Research, 45*(2), 165–190.

Halilovich, H. (2006). Aussie Bosnians from Germany: Reconstructing identity. *Local-*

Global: Identity, Security, Community, 2, 59–72.

Hermann, T. (2001).The impermeable identity wall: The study of violent conflicts by 'insiders' and 'outsiders'. In M. Smyth & G. Robinson G. (Eds), *Researching violently divided societies: Ethical and methodological issues* (pp. 77–91). Tokyo, Japan: United Nations University Press.

Hernandez Castillo, A.R. (2006). Fratricidal war or ethnocidal strategy? Women's experience with political violence in Chiapas. In V. Sanford & A. Angel-Ajani (Eds.), *Engaged observer: Anthropology, advocacy and activism* (pp. 149–169), New Brunswick, Canada: Rutgers University Press.

Hirsch, H. (1995). *Genocide and the politics of memory: Studying death to preserve life.* Chapel Hill: The University of Northern Carolina Press.

Hoare, M.A. (2003). Genocide in the former Yugoslavia: A critique of left revisionism's denial. *Journal of Genocide Research, 5*(4), 543–563.

Huyssen, A. (2003). *Present past: Urban palimpsests and the politics of memory.* Stanford, CA: Stanford University Press.

Jacobsen, K. & Landau, L.B. (2003). The dual imperative in refugee research: Some methodological and ethical considerations in social science research on forced migration. *Disasters, 27,* 185–206.

Johannsen, A. (2001). *Participatory action-research in post-conflict situations: The example of the war-torn societies project.* Berlin, Germany: Berghof Research Center for Constructive Conflict Management.

Kemmis, S. & McTaggart, R. (2000). Participatory action research. In N. Denzin and Y. Lincoln (Eds.), *The Handbook of qualitative research* (2nd ed., pp.559–604). London, England: Sage.

Krulfeld, R.M. (1998). Exploring new methods for collaboration in ethnographic research: An attempt at overcoming exploitation and violation of human rights. In Ruth M. Krulfeld & Jeffery, L. MacDonald (Eds.), *Power, ethics, and human rights: Anthropological studies of refugee research* (pp. 1–21). Lanham, MD: Rowman & Littlefield.

Lambert, M., Haasen, C. & Halilovich, H. (1998). Differential diagnosis of psychotic disorders in immigrants. *Psychiatrische Praxis, 25*(4), 198-199.

Liamputtong, P. & Ezzy, D. (2005). *Qualitative research methods* (2nd edition). Melbourne, Australia: Oxford University Press.

Mackenzie, C., McDowell, C. & Pittaway, E. (2007). Beyond 'Do no harm': the challenge of constructing ethical relationships in refugee research. *Journal of Refugee Studies, 20,* 299–319.

Madison, D.S. (2005). *Critical ethnography: Method, ethics and performance.* London: Sage Publications.

Marcus, G.E. (1998). *Ethnography through thick and thin.* Princeton, NJ: Princeton University Press.

Martin, S.F. (2000). Forced migration and the evolving humanitarian regime. *The UNHCR EPUA Working Papers, 20.*

McPherson, M., Horowitz, L.S., Lusher, D., di Giglio, S., Greenacre, L.E. & Saalmann, Y.B. (2011). Marginal women, marginal rights: Impediments to gender-based persecution claims by asylum-seeking women in Australia. *Journal of Refugee Studies, 24*(2), 347–348.

Nelson, R. (2011). Toward a history of rigour: An examination of the nasty side of scholarship. *Arts and Humanities in Higher Education, 10*(4), 375–388.

Nolin, C. (2006). *Transnational raptures: Gender and forced displacement.* Aldershot,

England: Ashgate.

O'Neill, M., Woods, P. & Webster, M. (2005). New arrivals: Participatory action research, imagined communities, and 'visions' of social justice. *Social Justice, 32*(1), 75–88.

Pittaway, E., Bartolomei, L. & Hugman, R. (2010). Stop stealing our stories: The ethics of research with vulnerable groups. *Journal of Human Rights Practice, 2*(2), 229–251.

Pui-Hing Wong, J. & Kwong-Lai Poon, M. (2010). Bringing translation out of the shadows: Translation as an issue of methodological significance in cross-cultural qualitative research. *Journal of Transcultural Nursing, 1*(21), 151-158.

Sanford, V. (2006). Excavations of the heart: Reflections on truth, memory, and structures of understanding. In V. Sanford & A. Angel-Ajani (Eds.), *Engaged observer: Anthropology, advocacy and activism* (pp. 1–19). New Brunswick, Canada: Rutgers University Press.

Smith, V.J. (2009). Ethical and effective ethnographic research methods: A case study with Afghan refugees in California. *Journal of Empirical Research on Human Research Ethics, 4*, 59–72.

Smyth, M. (2001). Introduction. In M. Smyth & G. Robinson G. (Eds), *Researching violently divided societies: Ethical and methodological issues* (pp. 12–33). Tokyo, Japan: United Nations University Press.

Stull, D.D. & Schensul, J.J. (1987). *Collaborative research and social change: Applied anthropology in action.* Hartford CT: The Institute for Community Research.

Summerfield, D. (2004). Cross cultural perspectives on the medicalisation of human suffering. In G. Rosen (Ed.), *Posttraumatic stress disorder: Issues and controversies* (pp. 233–246). Chichester, England: John Wiley.

Turton, D. (1996). Migrants and refugees: A Mursi case study. In T. Allen (Ed.), *In search of cool ground: war, flight & homecoming in northeast Africa* (pp. 96-110). Lawrenceville, NJ: Africa World Press.

Uehling, G. (1998). Is there 'refuge' in the refugee category? In R.M. Krulfeld & J.L. MacDonald (Eds.), *Power, ethics, and human rights anthropological studies of refugee research* (pp. 123–146). Lanham, MD: Rowman & Littlefield Publishers.

van de Port, M. (1999). It takes a Serb to know a Serb. *Critique of Anthropology, 19*(1), 7–30.

van der Velde, J. Deanna, L. Williamson, D.L. & Ogilvie, L.D. (2009). Participatory action research: Practical strategies for actively engaging and maintaining participation in immigrant and refugee communities. *Qualitative Health Research, 19*(9), 1293–1302.

van Willigen, J. (2002). *Applied anthropology: An introduction.* Westport, CT: Greenwood Publishing Group.

Voloder, L. (2008). Autoethnographic challenges: Confronting self, field and home. *The Australian Journal of Anthropology, 19*(1), 27–40.

CHAPTER

8

Doing Ethical Research: 'Whose Problem Is It Anyway?'

Eileen Pittaway and Linda Bartolomei

On starting work at a university after a career as an advocate based in the community sector, one of the authors, Pittaway, was challenged by a senior colleague who said, 'Well Eileen, you are now going to have to decide if you are an academic or an activist — what will it be?' This made her determined to demonstrate her belief that the most effective advocacy was that backed by solid academic research. In 1999 she was joined in this endeavour by fellow academic Linda Bartolomei. Their years of experience working with marginalised and often vulnerable refugee women and communities has consolidated their view that research conducted with such groups which does not have an advocacy outcome can be seen as unethical. However, the issue is complex. The strength of the advocacy depends on the rigour and validity of the research outcomes. The often unquestioned power which researchers have in research projects has to be questioned. The issue of representation has to be addressed. The field of refugee studies is one in which it is often difficult or impossible for refugees to represent themselves and they are therefore dependent on others to advocate on their behalf. The advocacy positions developed can at times reflect more of the belief systems and bias of the researchers than of those they are representing.

The methodology discussed in this chapter will examine a 'Participatory action research' methodology developed to address these issues. It is based on the belief that researchers working with extremely vulnerable populations must use research methods which enable them to conduct research in an ethical manner, while at the same time responding to the needs of the groups with whom they are working. The aim is to influence change at a legal, policy and service provision level, and to respect the inherent rights and dignity, knowledge and skills of research participants.

The model developed is a specific rights-based research methodology, designed to undertake advocacy-focused research that examines the issues in an ethical context, and is grounded in a human rights framework and a community-based participatory approach (Ife, 2009). It is designed for working with individuals experiencing multiple oppressions and persecution. The methodology addresses complex issues such as the ethics of undertaking research with vulnerable populations, and in particular the use of individual 'stories' as research data. These aspects of the methodology are mentioned in this paper but developed more fully in other papers by the authors (Hugman, Bartolomei, & Pittaway, 2011; Hugman, Pittaway, & Bartolomei, 2011; Mackenzie, McDowell, & Pittaway, 2007; Pittaway, Bartolomei, & Hugman, 2010). A critical concern of the methodology is to ensure that innovative methodologies produce academically rigorous outcomes and strong research impacts.

It is a 'work in progress', constantly evaluated and amended in consultation with refugee groups. We make no claims that it is a 'perfect solution', and we ourselves experience flaws and challenges in using it. However, it is a method that provides a good basis for advocacy. It has achieved significant research impacts, including changes in international law and UN policy and practice. It has influenced refugee-related policy in Australia, the UK and the US. For example, following work with the Rohingya refugee communities in Bangladesh and the production of a report with UNHCR Geneva (UNHCR, 2007) both Australia and the UK opened up a number of places within their resettlement programs specifically for Rohingya refugees from the camps in Bangladesh. The model is also respected by the refugee communities with whom we work. Importantly it is a model with which we feel ethically comfortable.

It began in 2001 when the authors were working with refugee groups on the Thai Burma border in preparation for a major UN Conference. The groups wished to advocate about their experiences of endemic rape and sexual abuse by the Burmese military and the impact of this on the women and their communities. Without consulting the refugee groups, we decided that research was needed into the issue and obtained funding to conduct it. To our surprise and humiliation, the refugee groups were at first unwilling to participate in the research project. They discussed the fact that they were tired of constant requests to participate in research projects by postgraduate students, international NGOs, and human rights groups, for which they perceived little or no direct benefit to the people who gave their time. They cited many cases when the disclosure put individuals and communities in danger. They alerted us to their distrust, fear and feeling of exploitation, which they had from involvement in research using more mainstream methodologies. Despite this, they recognised the need for their stories to be told for a number of complex reasons, including validation, healing, advocacy and action for change. They were in a double bind — that of wanting the outcomes, but distrusting the process. In discussing whether or not they would be prepared to engage with us in a research project, two issues became paramount. The first was, who has control of what is done with the data collected and the second was whether they and their communities would experience any benefit from participating with the researchers.

After lengthy negotiations, the refugee groups decided that they would work with the Centre for Refugee Research on a research project if these issues were addressed and this marked the beginning of the development of the methodology. The groups requested that human rights training be provided as part of the research process, and that they themselves be trained to undertake and to participate in their own research projects.

The particular concerns raised by the refugee groups on the Thai Burma border were feelings of having being exploited by researchers. The same issues have subsequently been discussed by refugees around the world. The issues included serious breaches of confidentiality, such as the unauthorised publication of names and photos, leading at times to situations of danger for those participating in the research.

> XX agency came and did a big report — it was very good, but they published it without asking us — people were thrown out of their houses, threatened — we are all afraid to speak now, it is worse than before. (Refugee man, India, 2010)

Another key issue was the lack of any feedback or outcomes for the time refugee groups invested in responding to researchers. This included never receiving the promised reports and photos after disclosing personal stories; and the feeling of abandonment when often horrendous malpractice or abuses were reported, with nothing done to address them.

> If we had a copy of every PhD, every report people had promised to send us — of every photo they had taken, this hut would be so full — so what do you see? Nothing! (Refugee woman, Thai-Burma Border, 2003)

> They take hours of the time of refugees and workers and do not even buy anything from the refugee craft shops. (NGO worker, Thai–Burma border, 2004)

> They cry about our stories but nothing changes — don't they ever try and help us after [they leave]? (Refugee Man, New Delhi, India, 2007)

Refugees also discussed their fear of backlash from government authorities and military leaders within camps if it is known they participate in research projects.

> At times we are too scared to take part even if we want to, because of what will happen after they have gone. (Rohingya refugees, Bangladesh, 2007)

> You can just get into your big white car and drive away the moment there is any danger — we have to stay and live with it. (Rohingya refugees, Bangladesh, 2007)

There was also a deep mistrust of researchers who have little or no cultural or political understanding of the circumstances in which the refugees live. There was a particular distrust of researchers who 'fly in and fly out' (Chambers, 1983, as cited in Harrell-Bond, 1986) of refugee sites and conflict zones without considering the local social economic and political consequences. They questioned the validity of data collected in this way.

> They have ideas about us but never ask us. We were in the forest for so long and in such hard times, no food, no water, by the time we got to the camp, we had no clothes left. Next thing people were being told that we were so backwards that we always go naked. (Refugee Woman, Sherkole, Ethiopia, 2005)

> After you had been here, some of the local workers told us there would be trouble because of what we had told you. They said there would be 'consequences'. (Refugee man, time and place withheld)

Increasingly, advocates and researchers are suggesting that modern technology such as mobile phones and videos be given to refugees to assist them to record abuses and issues of concern. While in some instances these strategies might be appropriate, often they are not. To the refugees they can demonstrate a lack of understanding on the part of researchers of the reality of refugee lives, which foster distrust and lack of confidence.

> don't you understand … we have no electricity, no computers, we are in huts deep in the forest, far from anything, no money for food — who will pay for the [SIM] cards? — you do not know us at all. (Refugee participant in a local town for a consultation, 2011)

Another concern raised by the refugees was concern for the mental health of the participants.

> Why should we introduce you [researchers] to women who are traumatised if you can do nothing to help them? Just getting them to tell you their story can bring all the pain back. (Refugee woman, Thai–Burma border, 2003)

> They [researchers] send long questionnaires about trauma to people without support and never follow up to see if it upset them. (Refugee man resettled to Australia, 2005)

A final group of concerns was about the way in which many researchers fail to recognise refugees' agency, experience, wisdom, analysis and problem solving abilities. This was summed up by a refugee in Cairo, who pleaded '*We have a voice — hear us*'. The positioning of the researcher as 'the expert' and the refugee as victim was a recurring theme.

> Why do you never ask us what we think, what to do — it is always just tell us your problems. (Refugee Man, Cairo 20007)

> They think we are stupid, that we cannot help ourselves — how do they think we survived this far? (Resettled Refugee woman, Sydney 2009)

However, refugees are not stupid, and have a very clear analysis of their role in the research industry. They also exercise their power and agency.

> Sometimes we just lie so that they will go away and leave us alone … we pretend that no one speaks English … we send them to another part of the camp looking for someone we know is not there. (Refugee woman, Thai–Burma border, 2003)

The challenge was to develop a model which acknowledges this power and agency in a way that is respectful, maintains the dignity and autonomy of the participants and gives back as much benefit as the researchers gain. This challenge is ongoing.

'Reciprocal research', or 'Community consultation', is flexible and responsive to the needs of the groups with whom we work. While strongly informed by input from the refugee groups living in refugee camps and towns along the Thai–Burma border, it has been adapted following input from refugee groups in India, Bangladesh and Sri Lanka, Kenya, Ethiopia and Australia. It also aims to address some of the many ethical dilemmas for researchers involved in working with vulnerable populations. These include the possibility of the researched population being overly compliant to the researchers, in the hope of some form of relief or solution to their problems (Campbell, Wunungmurra, & Nyomba, 2005). It also addresses the often superficial nature of data collected when researchers 'fly in and fly out' of difficult situations. The issue is complex and multifaceted, because of the often competing dynamics in refugee situations. Refugee camps and urban sites are places of desperation. There is seldom enough food, medical services are minimal, and education standards are poor. Violence is endemic, and rape and sexual and gender-based violence the experience of the majority of refugee women and girls. This can call into play the values or rigour of the 'ethics of consent' and confidentiality.

> Informed consent is a joke when there is no food, no proper inter-preters to read the legalistic forms we take. No security ... some-times it makes me feel sick to have to ask people. (UNSW Researcher, 2010)

Researchers, in particular researchers from rich developed countries, can exert a lot of power. They sometimes bring gifts or even financial contributions to the communities. There is an expectation, however ill founded, that outsiders just might be able to secure resettlement from the camp, or procure some much needed assistance for individual refugees.

I sometimes think that refugees in the most desperate situations would dance naked if I asked them to if they thought it would save their families! (UNSW Researcher, 2010)

The strong human desire to protect self and family can put refugees in a position of trying to please researchers, telling them what they want to hear even if it is not always the truth.

The role of service providers and community gatekeepers in deciding who can speak to researchers was also discussed by refugee groups as critical to the validity of research findings. 'They never ask us — just the refugee committees. Never the women!' (Refugee Woman Ethiopia, 2006). They discussed how often the service providers who ran the camps decided who would speak to researchers. These were usually community leaders, often self-appointed, who had a vested interest in maintaining good relationships with those in power. They were very clear that if researchers really wanted to know what was happening in camps and refugee sites, they had to find ways of getting beyond the 'gatekeepers' to the broader refugee community.

In presenting the story of the development of the methodology, we describe it more as an interactive process, rather than a static model, as it is constantly evolving and developing in response to the populations with whom we work. Likewise, our theoretical analysis and critique is iterative, as we constantly review and deepen our analysis and understanding of the process in which we are involved.

Reciprocal Research – An Evolving Methodology

'Reciprocal research' with community groups incorporates a triangulation of methods, including the provision of human rights and other training, structured group work and interviews. The outcomes include a rich source of data, an identification of issues of concern based around the theme of the research project, a situational analysis, identification of appropriate and realistic solutions and a strategic plan drawn up with the communities involved.

It is a 'step-by-step' process that starts with the provision of human rights training and any additional training as requested by the refugee groups. The notion of human rights based 'advocacy' is introduced with the participants. The roles and potential assistance which can be provided by the researchers are clearly articulated and discussed, and things that the researchers cannot do are clearly explained. The participants are given the choice of whether they want to engage in the process or not. This is usually done overnight to allow them to discuss the project with the community. If this is not possible participants are asked to discuss it during a lunch break.

Critical to the entire process is an ethical 'confidentiality agreement', in which the researchers ensure that all the materials collected remain the property of the participants and can only be used with their permission. If the notion of 'confidentiality' is not familiar to the participants, a role play or mime is used to engender discussion and agreement as to why this is necessary. An ethical framework including, but often expanding the University Ethics agreement, is negotiated with participants. A commitment is signed by the researchers at the beginning of each consultation, promising that no reports, stories, photographs or DVDs about the consultations, will be released until it has been signed off by nominated members of the groups. This involves sending materials back to the group who have participated in the consultations for approval. It is important for researchers who undertake this type of methodology to build this time into their project planning.

The training introducing the human rights framework provides a context to guide participants through an examination and articulation of issues of critical concern to their communities. This is done through discussion based on the role of the UN, and an introduction to human rights. The training uses a series of graphics based on the Universal Declaration of Human Rights, depicting both positive rights (i.e., what rights we should have; e.g., food, health service and education) and negative rights (such as our right not to be tortured). The human rights learning is reinforced with exercises, such as making a symbolic human rights necklace that represents civil and political rights as well as social, cultural and economic rights. By including a bead for each set of rights, and forming a closed loop, this demonstrates the indivisibility and inalienability of human rights.

> The way we live now we have only problems. I do not have a human rights necklace and no-one listens to us.
>
> If I have a human rights necklace, the powerful people in big buildings will hear us, they will help us and our lives will improve. (Internally displaced woman, Colombia)

The use of graphics rather than written materials ensures that the training is accessible to people who are preliterate and is relatively easy to use in circumstances where professional interpreters are not always available. The researchers carry a data projector if a generator is available and use laminated posters when there is no electricity.

> I have been to human rights training before but it was nothing — we felt angry. This way is so good — I am thinking that you must have lived in Africa to know African people so well - you know how to talk with us, how we think. (Refugee woman, Zambia, 2011)

The second step uses a technique called 'story circles' (or stories as evidence) in which participants are invited to share stories of particular problems they have identified that are then positioned within the human rights framework. These can be their own stories, stories of friends, family or community members. This invitation provides participants with a degree of safety and a space in which, if they chose to, can share information without necessarily identifying the story as their own. The stories yield a large amount of rich data on the types of problems being experienced and the impact of these on individuals, families and communities. The aim of the story circles is to gather data and start the analysis of individual human rights abuses.

Table 8.1

Strategies Devised, Based on Analysis of Methodology, to Address the Issues of Concern

Strategies	Issue of Concern
Establishment of a meaningful confidentiality agreement with refugee groups, including clearly explaining what the researchers bring to the table, and what they can and cannot do and what they will gain from the process.	• Lessens fear of exploitation and leaves ownership of their stories with the refugee groups. • Provides an environment in which trust can be fostered, although refugees will only fully trust the process once researchers have fulfilled their promises.
Provision of accessible human rights and other training to provide a context for consultations and interviews	• The provision of training is seen by the majority of refugee groups as a resource which they highly value and they therefore perceive from the outset that there is a level of reciprocity in the relationship with the researchers. • Frank and open discussions of rights, responsibilities and the problems experienced in obtaining these, further create a trusting relationship. Training allows researchers to reach a wider number of people in the community than those who would often be nominated to take part in a research project.
Story Circles	• The use of story circles and treating stories as evidence validates the experiences of participants and allows them to disclose and explain their experiences in a way that interviews sometimes cannot. • The fact that the stories are presented as evidence of the issues discussed in the human rights training establishes a framework, which encourages participants to be frank about the abuses they are facing rather than sanitising or exaggerating their experiences to please the researcher.
Storyboards	• The storyboard process acknowledges that refugees have agency, experience, knowledge and wisdoms which can inform the analysis of their problems and generate meaningful solutions. • The process can assist refugees to move from absolute desperation to active participants in problem solving for themselves and their communities. It can in part address the power imbalance between researchers and refugees.
Strategic planning, advocacy to address the issues identified, and follow up actions	• This process enables refugees to take some control over their lives, however small, and to advocate on their own behalf. • Reports that come out of the training and consultations are owned and used by the refugee groups as well as by the researchers. New services and responses from UNHCR and NGOs have also occurred because of the issues identified by the refugees.
Meetings or communication with relevant service providers and other stakeholders	• The opportunity to meet or communicate with key stakeholders also acknowledges the agency of refugees, and is often the first opportunity that those apart from the community leaders have had to put forward their points of view.

As an alternative to story circles, in 2010 the authors, working with the UNHCR Gender Unit Geneva, devised a matrix exercise. One axis of the matrix lists 10 major issues of concern, these include access to registration, livelihoods, education, health services, shelter and protection from sexual and gender-based violence, and on the other axis, the life stages of refugee women, from babies to old women, and special needs groups such as unaccompanied minors, women with a disability and single headed households. In small groups participants discuss the impact of protection failures in each of the areas, and for different groups of women and girls. This exercise produced an enormous amount of invaluable data, and also solicited stories in just about every box of the matrix. Participants write their issues on 'Post-it' notes and place them in the appropriate boxes on the matrix as they discuss the problems they are experiencing.

The third step is to move from a focus on the problem to an analysis of the issue and identifying potential solutions. This involves a technique called 'storyboarding' in which participants use a series of drawings to conduct situational analyses including proposals for action, response and interventions. Working in small groups they are invited to focus on one of the key issues of concern that has arisen from the stories, and to prepare a series of six posters which analyse the issues. The posters can be either drawings, a mix of text and drawing, or collages of pictures taken from magazines. The focus is not on artistic ability, but on presenting a clear message to be presented to the larger groups. The posters illustrate six key questions:

1. The nature of the problem.
2. The impact of the problem on individuals, families, communities.
3. What is currently available to assist, and gaps in service provision.
4. Identification of potential solutions. (*If you were in charge of service provision for this issue, what would you do?*)

5. Identification of individuals or groups who might be able to assist.

6. The hoped-for outcome of the action.

The questions that inform each of the storyboards can be altered to suit the needs of particular groups and projects.

The storyboard technique allows participants to name problems and issues within their communities in a positive and empowering context. It recognises the skills, knowledge and experience that participants bring to situations, and provides a human rights framework, which acknowledges their rights to a secure life, and social support. The underlying premise is that all people have capabilities and capacity to identify and address community problems if the resources are available to support them.

An optimum use of the method occurs when the researched community is given the opportunity to present the outcomes of the consultations to service providers, NGOs and other people in power. The storyboards are an excellent basis for these presentations. Often this is the first time that the researched group will have had the opportunity to interact with those who have power over their lives as equals in a dialogue.

Key to the success of the methodology is the verbatim documentation of the issues identified in the human rights training, the stories and the commentary given by participants when describing their storyboards. The feedback and clarification undertaken by the facilitator and the discussion by the larger group of each presentation is also recorded. This forms a major source of data collection and can be analysed either manually or with social sciences computer software. Interviews can be undertaken to further explore themes that emerge from the analysis of the documentation.

The establishment of trust between the researcher and the group with whom they are working is critically important. Researchers are often time and resource poor, which can be prerequisites for establishing this trust. One method used by the centre to quickly establish a relationship which we have found promotes trust has been the use of a DVD of previous consultations. Once groups, even those displaying some obvious reluctance, have been shown a video of previous consultations with other groups, they quickly agree to engage in the process, usually requesting that a DVD be made of their own consultation. In all cases to date, that initial trust has quickly grown because of the process itself, enabling the sharing of in-depth stories as testimonies and evidence.

Through the use of this methodology, we have not only developed an understanding of the risks and problems facing refugees but provided a framework from which to identify and develop solutions. This represented a significant and lasting shift in approach, in which the research was conducted not *about*, but *with* the refugee communities. These were 'bottom up' processes, which started with the realities, lived experience and problems as they were articulated and prioritised by the refugee communities (Briggs & Sharp, 2004; Rahnema, 2001).

Analysis of the Methodology

Table 8.1 (see p. 161) provides an analysis of how the methodology addresses the concerns raised by refugees and researchers.

It has been demonstrated that the process gives participants a space to share information that they have previously withheld. The outcomes provide a rich and thorough analysis of the issues of concern and the experiences of the communities. It details their analysis of the situation and their suggestions for change. It is a genuine community development process which positions the stories and experiences of the participants in a sociopolitical context (Herman, 1992; Tesoriero, 2010).

Discussion

The methodology outlined in this chapter, has its roots in action research, which according to Reason and Bradbury (2006):

> seeks to bring together action, reflection, theory and practice in participation with others, in the pursuit of practical solutions

to issues of pressing concern to people, and more generally the flourishing of individual persons and their communities. (p. 1)

To this end Kurt Lewin's exhortation in 1946 that 'Research that produces nothing but books will not suffice' (as cited in Smith, 2001, p. 12) continues to frame action research methods and approaches today.

Reason and Bradbury (2006) suggest that the conduct of good action research is predicated upon the researcher clearly articulating choices relating to design, method and actions in the conduct of the research. It is extremely difficult to build trust with vulnerable populations from the position of an objective observer. To do this the researcher has to engage directly in the issues of concern to the research participants (Reason & Bradbury, 2006, p. 1). It is also predicated on the willing involvement of those people participating in the activity under research.

> They will only come the first day because they have been told to — these meetings take them away from working in the fields — they think it is a waste of time! (NGO service provider, time and place withheld)

> We came [on the first day] because there was food — we did not want to — but when you started talking about human rights it was different — by the end of the day we had a discussion and we decided we wanted to work with you. (Refugee participant, time and place withheld)

This varies from other methods which regard the people involved in the activity as subjects to be observed, rather than equal participants in the research/process of change. It is this balance of power which is crucial to the success of action research and is also one of the most difficult aspects to achieve. Researchers do bring power into a situation. Power of knowledge, of resources and the power of being the person or people officially charged with or acknowledged as agents of change. Therefore, the way in which this potential power imbalance is handled is imperative to a successful research outcome (Grant, Nelson, & Mitchell, 2008, p. 592.)

Transformative participation is the principle of power sharing between researchers and participants in the identification and development of local knowledge. Consultations are based on 'emancipatory pedagogy' (Freire, 1970) and critically examine existing approaches, ensuring that the participants are developing and shaping interventions that they perceive to be relevant. Its premise is that all people have capabilities and capacity to identify and address community problems if the resources are available to support them. The monitoring of the ethical aspects process is an ongoing activity during the project.

The epistemological approach underlying the methodology is that of constructionism. It asserts that there are no objective truths waiting to be discovered but that instead, knowledge and meaning are constructed and co-constructed through the interaction of the researcher and the research participants (Crotty, 1998; Denzin & Lincoln, 2000). This is a view of knowledge which challenges the privileging of expert and professional knowledge over lay knowledge. It accepts the view that knowledge, and meaning 'is contingent upon human practices, being constructed in and out of interaction between human beings and their world, and developed and transmitted within an essentially social context' (Crotty, 1998, p. 43). It is a useful tool for research-based advocacy, as each party brings a specific set of skills and knowledge to the table. The world-view and values of the researcher are acknowledged and negotiated as some of the shaping forces of the research and the advocacy outcomes.

A major strength of this methodology is that it actively involves participants in a sophisticated situational analysis, enabling effective identification of a range of appropriate strategies to address issues of concern and needs that emerge during consultations. It reflects a belief in the existing capacity and skills of participants to identify and analyse issues of concern, to develop appropriate and achievable responses, to identify existing service provision and strengths, to identify service gaps and failures. We argue that it fulfils the aim of conducting rigorous academic research, leading to positive social change in an ethical manner. At the same time, because of the uniqueness of the situation and the complexity of the social and political issues involved it also allows the researchers to uncover findings that would have remained hidden if a more conventional methodology was employed.

Research Limitations

It could be argued that in some ways this methodology also has the potential to be coercive. It has been found that refugees across the world are desperate for training, so the offer of training in return for involvement in the research has proven to be a very popular option. It could therefore be suggested that the refugees are 'co-opted' into the research process through their need for training. It could be argued that using training as part of the research process was in some way deceiving participants, for example, some men will allow the women to attend training on livelihoods but would not let them take part in a research project. We believe that the ethical procedure put into place and the negotiated nature of the process, and the guaranteed control of the content of reports produced by the researchers goes a long way to addressing these concerns. There have been a few occasions when refugees have requested that reports be withheld, or that sections be removed from reports and this has been done.

This is not a quick and easy form of research. The research team has to be able to dedicate at least two weeks for the groups to be consulted, with significant preparation and follow up. The research team need to establish relationships with gatekeepers and community-based groups with whom they wish to work and this can still pose a problem. The researchers need to establish a working relationship with the refugee community before they undertake the training in order to negotiate what particular types of training the groups may need additional to the human rights training. The research team has to have a range of training materials available to them, in order to respond to the needs of the groups with whom they work. Training offered by the authors include advocacy training, income generation and livelihood training, an introduction to counselling skills, young women's leadership training and ways of including men in the protection of women from sexual and gender-based violence. While this might sound formidable, the quantity and quality of data collected during the six steps of the process is sometimes overwhelming and much richer and more detailed than that which could be collected using more traditional methodologies.

Conclusion

Based on these principles, it is argued that the methodology facilities the collection of information from often vulnerable populations in a way that is empowering, not harmful or exploitative, and which has the potential for bringing about social change. This makes it an ideal tool for research-based advocacy. The reciprocal nature of the method transforms people from subjects of research to participants in research, moves from 'harm minimisation' as an ethical base to reciprocal benefit and from researcher directed projects and outcomes, to participants and community directed outcomes (Pittaway & Bartolomei, 2008).

The methodology is ideal for use with marginalised and disadvantaged groups who have valid and historically based reasons for distrusting people in authority, including researchers, academics and representatives of government and other institutions. This might include people who experience discrimination on the basis of such things as class, race, gender, disability, or refugee status. If rigorously used, it can ensure that any advocacy that is based on the research reflects the outcomes required by the participants, not only those of the researchers, addressing a question asked by one refugee, 'whose problem is it anyway?'

References

Briggs, J., & Sharp, J. (2004). Indigenous knowledge and development: A postcolonial caution. *Third World Quarterly, 25*(4), 661–676.

Campbell, D., Wunungmurra, P., & Nyomba, H. (2005). Starting where the people are: Lessons on community development from a remote Aboriginal Australian setting. *Community Development Journal, 42*(2), 151–166.

Crotty, M. (1998). *The foundations of social research: Meaning and perspectives in the research process.* Sydney, Australia: Allen and Unwin.

Denzin, N.K., & Lincoln, Y.S. (2000). *Handbook of qualitative research* (2nd ed.). Thousand Oaks, CA: Sage.

Dyregrov, K., Dyregrov, A,. & Raudalen, M. (2000). Refugee families' experience of research participation. *Journal of Traumatic Stress, 13*(3), 413–426.

Fals Borda, O. (2001). Participatory (action) research in social theory: Origins and challenges. In P. Reason & H. Bradbury (Eds.), *Handbook of action research* (2nd ed., pp. 27–32). London, England: Sage.

Freire, P. (1970). *Pedagogy of the oppressed.* New York, NY: Continuum.

Grant, J., Nelson, G., & Mitchell, T. (2008). Negotiating the challenges of participatory action research: Relationships, power, participation, change and credibility. In P. Reason & H. Bradbury (Eds.). *The Sage handbook of action research, participative enquiry and practice* (pp. 589–601). London, England: Sage.

Harrell-Bond, B.E. (1986). *Imposing aid: Emergency assistance to refugees.* Oxford, England: Oxford University Press.

Herman, J.L. (1992). *Trauma and recovery.* New York, NY: Basic Books.

Hugman, R., Bartolomei, L., & Pittaway, E. (2011). Human agency and the meaning of 'informed consent': Reflections on research with refugees. *Journal of Refugee Studies, 24*, 656–671.

Hugman, R., Pittaway, E., & Bartolomei, L. (2011). When 'do no harm' is not enough: The ethics of research with refugees and other vulnerable groups. *British Journal of Social Work, 41*, 1271–1287.

Ife, J. (2009). *Human rights from below: Achieving rights through community development.* Cambridge, England: Cambridge University Press.

Lewis, H.M. (2001). Participatory research and education for social change: Highlander Research and Education Centre. In P. Reason & H. Bradbury (Eds.), *Handbook of action research* (2nd ed., pp. 262–268). London, England: Sage.

Mackenzie, C., McDowell, C., & Pittaway, E. (2007). Beyond 'do no harm': The challenge of constructing ethical relationships in refugee research. *Journal of Refugee Studies, 20*(2), 299–319.

Pittaway, E., & Bartolomei, L. (2008, Autumn). Reciprocal research by community consultation. *Refugee Transitions, 21*(2).

Pittaway, E., Bartolomei, L., & Hugman, R. (2010). 'Stop stealing our stories': The ethics of research with vulnerable groups. *Journal of Human Rights Practice, 2*(2), 229–251.

Rahnema, M. (2001). Participation. In W. Sachs (Ed.), *The development dictionary* (pp. 116–31). Johannesburg, South Africa: Witwatersrand University Press.

Reason, P., & Bradbury, H. (2006). *Handbook of action research (2nd ed.).* London, England: Sage.

Smith, M.K. (2001). Kurt Lewin: Groups, experiential learning and action research. *The encyclopaedia of informal education* (pp.1–15). Retrieved from http://www.infed.org/thinkers/et-lewin.htm

Tesoriero, F. (2010). *Community development: community-based alternatives in an age of globalization* (4th ed.). Sydney, Australia: Pearson Education.

United Nations High Commissioner for Refugees. (2007) *Refugee consultations — Bangladesh*. Retrieved from http://www.unhcr.org/refworld/docid/46f0ec002.html

Winter, R. (1998). Finding a voice — thinking with others: A conception of action research. *Educational Action Research, 6*(1), 53–68.

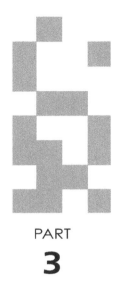

PART
3

ADVOCACY AND POLITICS
—
CONSIDERING THE RAMIFICATIONS OF RESEARCH

CHAPTER

9

Researching Immigration Detention: Documenting Damage and Ethical Dilemmas

Louise Newman

Mandatory detention of asylum seekers in Australia continues to be a focus of debate and concern. Mandatory detention, which applies to all so-called unauthorised arrivals, was introduced in 1992, and has impacted on more than 20,000 people since. Under immigration law it requires that all asylum seekers arriving without documentation be detained in designated security facilities. Detention is arbitrary and indefinite and applies to both children and adults. While detention is said to be for administrative purposes, such as health and security checks, it is also seen by government to have significant deterrent value and to be sending a message that unauthorised arrival does not result in freedom or straightforward entry into Australia. More recently, it is proposed that asylum seekers will receive no processing of their claims in Australia and will be sent to another country such as Malaysia where their claims for asylum may be heard. This raises the issue of Australia's obligations as a voluntary signatory to the UNHCR Refugee Convention as well as concerns about its broader commitment to advocacy for human rights and protection in the Asian region. Immigration detention, therefore, serves both local and regional political agendas and has become a focus of national discussion.

One reason why Australia's detention regime has been controversial is that it has had the effect of isolating asylum seekers. Detention facilities have been developed and continue to be built in remote parts of the country where service provision and access to health and mental health services are problematic. Of concern, visiting and external scrutiny is also more difficult in remote areas and the impact of the facilities on small local communities is significant. The decision to excise off-shore islands from the migration zone also created a system of remote processing for asylum seekers and placed limitations on legal support and appeal processes. While the aim of government might be seen as one of limiting inappropriate and protracted legal processes, the net result of this system was arguably lack of representation and violations of rights to legal advice and claims. On another level, offshore processing has served to render the plight of asylum seekers invisible and removed from the general community conscience.

The reality of the desperate needs of asylum seekers has received little media coverage and has allowed for the ongoing rhetoric of border protection, and raising of anxiety among some sections of the community. Limited numbers of unauthorised arrivals have been portrayed in the media as a significant threat and one that must be managed in the strictest sense. Government has focused on deterring asylum seekers. The fundamental assumption here is that unauthorised arrivals bypass available process for determining refugee status, voluntarily put themselves and others at risk and have no regard for the needs of those who may be more deserving of protection. This simplistic and anxiety provoking discourse has militated against more reflective assessment of the reasons behind and impact of asylum seeking — the motives, ambivalence and psychological consequences of loss and displacement are not often part of political coverage of the issues. It is in this context that psychological research has played a significant part in the 'asylum seeker debate' and continues to raise key issues of ethical and human rights commitment.

Research into the operation and impact of mandatory detention on asylum seekers' mental health raises fundamental clinical and ethical dilemmas. Asylum seekers are a vulnerable population with high levels of pre-existing vulnerability and traumatic experiences. They then find themselves within a complex and often confusing legal system that may be very different in terms of cultural understanding. Concepts of research, and the needs of researchers to study and document harm and distress, cannot be seen as unproblematic in this context. The ethical challenges in this arena are the focus of this chapter and include the need to protect vulnerable groups, the use of research findings for purposes of political advocacy and the challenges raised when research findings are questioned by government for specific policy objectives.

In reviewing research findings on mandatory detention, it is also important to consider the relationships that develop between research 'subjects', in this case detainees and those who research them, and the boundaries around research, advocacy and personal involvement. Research in this area also involves associates such as interpreters, community workers and the individuals with joint roles as researchers and members of particular cultural groups. The personal impact of research in this area has had scant attention despite the complexity of the issues.

Research Challenges

Given the complex political context, researchers must grapple with the issue of 'neutrality' and the need to engage in social debate. Researching asylum seekers and documenting high rates of suffering and mental health problems, by definition, makes a commentary on systems of detention and health care for this population. In practice, as is outlined below, research findings in Australia became contested by government, seized on by advocates and those questioning mandatory detention and were of great significance in the debate. Researchers and clinicians found themselves in the position of working at the interface of political advocacy and the academy.

Researchers and clinicians became involved in the detention debates in increasing numbers during the operation of remote facilities in Woomera and Baxter in South Australia where behavioural disturbances, riots and suicidal behaviour became endemic. High levels of distress and despair and a dysfunctional and punitive system of detention resulted in mass protest and self-harm. The impact of this on children and the detention of over 3,000 children during this period raised community concern and protest. Cases of children with severe psychiatric disturbance and developmental problems were publicised and heightened concern about the detention system contributed to damage and disturbance. Researchers found themselves in the middle of a highly politicised environment where psychological findings were discussed in parliament and attempts were made to discredit research teams and ignore clear and robust results. For the researchers this forced an engagement with the ethics of doing research on detained populations where government may not wish to know the results and the more complex issue of how to support detainees in this context. Concepts of neutrality and minimal self-disclosure became problematic and the personal impact of this work on the researchers involved was significant. Processes for support and case review were developed and reflection on our own roles was central. Research and advocacy for human rights are seen as inseparable and the dissemination of results was clearly involved in a political process. There were varying levels of comfort with a politicised research agenda among professional groups and also a degree of concern about the possible consequences of questioning the policy of mandatory detention and immigration policy. This concern continues currently given that there has been no move towards removal of mandatory detention from the Immigration Act despite policy changes supporting community detention alternatives for some groups such as children and unaccompanied minors.

Research has focused on the impact of experiences in detention on vulnerable groups of asylum seekers and also on modelling the factors contributing to better or worse outcome. Factors such as length of time in detention, negative experiences and traumatic exposure, and the process of establishing refugee claims are all significant components of the asylum seeking experience. The role of pre-existing trauma and impact of persecution, displacement and loss also contribute to risk and mediate outcomes. The specific needs of children and vulnerability in the face of trauma and detention have also been examined. These studies have raised issues of the meaning of individual diagnosis and formulation of difficulties when the environment of detention and the refugee determination process itself is a major factor in producing distress. This of course raises the issue of what sort of psychological treatment will be useful if the individual remains in a situation where recovery is not possible. The 'toxic environment' of the detention centre with its often dysfunctional culture and priorities acts to increase distress and confusion, and overall rates of mental health problems. The example of a psychologist teaching 'anger management' following a protest action among a group of distressed detainees is a case where psychological principles do not refer to context or understand the healthy role of political protest for persecuted individuals.

Following enquiries into the running of detention centres, significant changes in approach were attempted with the development of a Detention Health framework and a new approach to the provision of mental health services. This has been an attempt to reduce risk, provide support for detainees during the process and acknowledge that detention itself can have negative impact on health and wellbeing. The designation of detainees as 'clients' and the establishment of case managers and the description of the 'journey' of those in detention is in one sense positive but has also served to obscure the fact that these are involuntary clients with significant risk of mental deterioration. Increasing length of time in detention, slowing of processing and detention of those with histories of torture and trauma has again produced a high risk and volatile situation with increasing rates of self-harm and clusters of suicidal behaviour and completed suicides. Research conducted from 2000 that has found a clear relationship between detention and mental disorder has again become part of a political discussion. The importance of documenting harm and the impact of government policy has again become a priority. Professional bodies and clinicians are again facing complex issues of attempting to advise government of the risks of maintaining the policy of mandatory detention and the long-term consequences in terms of health and social functioning of those eventually released. Ethical issues, professional roles and research have again become prominent in the current debate.

Detention and Mental Health

Mental health professionals have played a major part in raising clinical and ethical concerns regarding the impact of mandatory detention and particularly its impact on child development. For many clinicians the need to intervene and advocate on behalf of detainees raised serious questions about the boundaries of professional behaviour and the moral responsibility to oppose damaging government policy even at some degree of individual risk. Gathering evidence about the mental health impacts of detention became an important strategy in this debate, yet even this was opposed by the government of the day who accused researchers of bias. The relationship between mental health and human rights was brought into focus by the findings of several studies that detention and lack of resolution of refugee status undermine psychological wellbeing and contribute to ongoing deterioration.

The prolonged nature of detention with associated uncertainty about the future and persistent anxiety is regarded as a major contributing factor to mental deterioration, depression and increasing hopelessness. Early studies found an association between length of time in detention and the severity of mental disorder (Sultan & O'Sullivan, 2001), a finding supported by later research (Steel et al., 2004). In this context, self-harm is simultaneously a form of protest and an expression of frustration and sometimes of suicidal ideation. Several reports noted high rates of self-harm among detainees and forms of symbolic protest such as mouth sewing. The question of suicidal intent is often difficult to assess and the detention system has tended to label all such behaviour as 'manipulative' and lacking in serious intent, ignoring the ambivalence and complex feelings involved. Government at the time denied any association between the conditions of detention and protest behaviour and mental distress and reiterated that this behaviour related to manipulation and was a sign of poor character. The clear lack of understanding of the psychological implications of asylum seeking within a punitive system were apparent, and also the difficulty in acknowledging the reality of mental distress and need for support. 'Bad not mad' became the refrain of a government very much opposed to looking at the environmental contribution to this mental distress and deterioration (Dudley, 2003).

Between July and December 2001 there were 688 major incidents involving 1,149 detainees across the detention system. 174 were of significant self-harm and 23 involved children. Several reports noted the damaging impact on children of witnessing self-harm and suicidal behaviour and particularly the impact of witnessing the deterioration of family members. The 2004 *Human Rights and Equal Opportunities Commission Report* on children in detention noted the negative developmental effects of detention on children and the failure of the Australian Government to respect its obligations under international human rights treaties it has subscribed to. It also noted the potential long-term effects of traumatic exposure with the risk of ongoing mental disorder. The report noted the difficulties faced by parents in the detention environment and the way in which parental depression and despair affected children resulting in attachment difficulties. Several clinical reports describe children with attachment disorders, socially indiscriminate behaviour and developmental delay. The lack of care and protection and appropriate activities for play and education were also criticised. As well as this environmental deprivation children were exposed to behavioural disturbance, violence and self-harm. Older children and adolescents were involved in protest behaviour and younger children were witnesses to this with inadequate protection. Clinicians and child workers played a key role in highlighting this situation as one of extreme risks to children and unacceptable under several international conventions and child protection frameworks.

The case of 'SB', a 5-year-old Iranian child in detention with his family, received considerable public attention and raised community awareness of the plight of detained children. SB was held in Woomera for an 11-month period and was exposed to riots, self-harming behaviours and suicide attempts. He was described as becoming withdrawn and anxious and having nightmares. The family was transferred to the Villawood centre in New South Wales where he witnessed a significant suicide attempt and become withdrawn and mute, deteriorating to a state where he refused all oral intake and was hospitalised. SB required several admissions for rehydration and every time he was returned to the detention facility his condition deteriorated. He was assessed by several child psychiatrists, who all made the point that returning the child to such a traumatic environment would result in relapse and advising that he should be released into the community with his mother. This was declined by the then minister for immigration who was concerned that this would set a precedent for the release of children from detention! Predictably SB's condition deteriorated and he was removed from the centre and placed in community foster care separated from his mother. As he continued to deteriorate his mother was released 4 months after separation and his father 8 months later. SB was found to be a genuine Convention refugee. He remains distressed with features of posttraumatic stress disorder (PTSD) and is under ongoing treatment of adjustment difficulties, depression and trauma symptoms.

SB's case was an example of harm to a child resulting from inflexible government policy where clinicians felt they had an obligation to be open about the child's plight and to act as advocates. Advocacy was not seen as in conflict with, or separate from, the role of being a clinician. This position was not accepted by the minister of the day, who queried whether a psychiatrist could also be an advocate for the rights of a child and implied that there was a conflict inherent in arguing for the release of a detained child on medical grounds. The whole question of the nature of medical and psychiatric recommendation about treatment and placement of detainees became very difficult, with clinicians arguing that in some cases the environmental contribution to disorder was so great that the only possibility of 'recovery' lay in release and community placement. In some cases government accused detainees of simulating illness and psychiatric condition to gain release and failed to acknowledge the reality of psychological distress.

These situations raise fundamental ethical demands for clinicians and medical practitioners attempting to care for vulnerable clients. The doctor/clinician has a duty of care to the individual and a duty to advocate for necessary treatment and support. The issues of location of treatment and the direct impact of detention and health became highly contested with government arguing that Migration law took priority over health concerns. Researchers engaged directly in this debate by a focus on producing evidence that this approach was fundamentally damaging.

The response of the detention system to individuals seen as simulating psychiatric disturbance was highlighted by the case of 'CR', an Australian permanent resident found to have been held unlawfully in detention for a period of 10 months. CR was suffering from a severe and chronic psychotic disorder and was acutely unwell and speaking her native language (German) when she was detained, initially in prison and then in immigration detention as it was assumed that she was an 'illegal' person. Her condition deteriorated and she was housed in a behavioural management unit, largely in isolation. She became behaviourally disorganised to the point that she was incoherent, smearing faeces and removing her clothes. Despite this, the detention system did not recognise this as possible mental illness and she did not receive adequate psychiatric assessment or any treatment. CR was treated as 'badly behaved' and disruptive and was only released to care when recognised by family members in a media article. Ironically, fellow detainees recognised that CR was mentally unwell and had asked for her to be assessed and cared for in a psychiatric facility. This case raised serious issues about the culture of the detention system, which focuses on behavioural control and repeatedly questioned the motives of detainees, including their supposed attempts to be manipulative and deceitful. The Palmer report that followed this incident looked at the provision of mental health services and support in detention and stressed the need for ongoing independent monitoring of service standards and provision of appropriate levels of care. This report prompted the establishment of an independent advisory body comprising representatives of medical and health professional bodies (Detention Expert Health Advisory Group, 2005), which continues to function to provide advice to the Department regarding the health and mental health needs of asylum seekers and detainees' suicidal ideation.

Clinical Research

There is now a considerable body of scientific research demonstrating consistent findings of high rates of mental disorder in detained asylum seekers. These findings point to the negative impact of detention and the way in which detention directly contributes to the development of mental disorder. Undertaking this research raises fundamental issues as to the capacity of detainees to relate to the implications of revealing details of their experiences to groups outside the system and the limitations of any study in terms of influencing outcome for detainees in an immediate and positive sense. There is also the question of the need to repeat the documentation of harm in different groups when it may be the case that the harm of detention in a generic sense has already been established. There is a clear need to understand the vulnerability of detainees as research participants and to think through the ethical issues raised by this research agenda.

Detainees frequently express distress at their powerless position and the prevailing culture of disbelief and blame in detention centres. Asylum seekers have made an active and often difficult decision to leave home, culture and family and for unaccompanied minors the burden of carrying on their culture and future is significant. To find that the system is one of rules and bureaucratic regulation which erode individual autonomy and sense of control is deeply disturbing and unexpected. Unrealistic wishes about rapid processing and release may compound this situation where the asylum seeker feels powerless and abandoned. For survivors of torture and trauma the situation is even more serious and distressing as a result of what is experienced as a traumatising regime. Traumatic responses may be triggered by unempathic, intrusive and rigid responses to high levels of distress and anxiety. In these situations encounters between staff and asylum seekers can become conflictual and come to represent anger and sense of frustration towards the immigration system.

Silove and colleagues (2006) studied 10 of 11 families in a remote centre using standardised instruments for diagnostic assessment. Every adult was found to have major depression and most reported suicidal ideation. All children were diagnosed with at least one psychiatric disorder and most met diagnostic criteria for more than one disorder. Half the children had PTSD and separation anxiety disorder and more than half expressed suicidal ideation. A quarter of the children had engaged in self-harm. Assessment of lifetime prevalence of mental disorder found a low level of pre-existing psychiatric symptoms or disorder, again supporting the view that detention itself has psychiatric consequences. A striking feature of this study was the high reporting of negative experiences within the detention system including abusive and harsh treatment and witnessing self-harm and suicidal behaviour. This article contributed to a program of advocating for the removal of vulnerable children and individuals from detention and calls for the abolition of mandatory detention.

Length of time in detention has emerged as a major contributing factor to mental deterioration, physical symptoms and hopelessness. An early study by a detained medical practitioner in Villawood detention centre (Sultan & O'Sullivan, 2001) found that severity of depressive symptoms increased with the length of time in detention and deteriorated to a state of cognitive deficit, pervasive mistrust and psychotic symptoms. A major concern remains that there is a lack of understanding of the deterioration as related to detention and an assumption that these conditions are responsive to treatment within detention and without resolution of the individual's status.

Recent work reviewing medical records of detainees again finds that length of time is related to health problems and particularly notes complex physical health presentations, medical service utilisation and mental health diagnoses increasing at the 12-month period. Rates of disorder are low in the early periods of detention and extremely high after 18 months in detention

(Green & Eagar, 2010). While this relationship and risk are now accepted by government, it remains difficult to maintain only brief periods of detention (current policy of 90 days) and to facilitate community processing of particularly vulnerable groups such as survivors of torture and children. On the basis of the evidence, community alternatives to detention, if based on a model of personal autonomy and participation, may be the only way to prevent deterioration and increasing distress and rates of self-harm. The occurrence of 5 suicides across the detention system from September 2010 to July 2011 is extremely concerning and requires rethinking of the policy of mandatory detention.

The research outlined above has played a significant role in the 'asylum seeker' debate and calls for reform of immigration law in Australia. The results have been used to counter the prevailing tendency to deny or minimise the negative impact of detention and to point to high levels of psychiatric morbidity arising from detention experiences. Asylum seekers do of course arrive with traumatic exposure and pre-existing high levels of traumatic exposure and loss, which will also impact rates of distress, but research suggests that it is the experience of detention itself that is most significant. This raises issues of the capacity to provide 'treatment' in this environment and for clinicians can result in a feeling of disempowerment and lack of skill. Reassurance, simplistic approaches to dealing with anger and frustration and depression have limited utility, particularly where self-harm and behavioural disturbance have been seen as politically motivated 'bad behaviour'. This has resulted in under-recognition of serious mental distress and disorder, difficulty in creating a more psychologically supportive environment and conditions that may actually increase distress and disorder. Treating professionals have little control over the length of time an asylum seeker spends in detention and are often in the position of observing deterioration with very little in the way of intervention to influence this. The limitations of the traditional clinical role are evident and place clinicians in a position where ethical dilemmas are unavoidable. The age-old question of whether to work within or to oppose from without may polarise the options but remains significant.

Clinical and Ethical Dilemmas

As mentioned above many clinicians have described feelings of lack of efficacy in dealing with detained populations. Advocacy or speaking on behalf of those with little power and maintaining a stance of support for the best interests of the detainee becomes important in a situation where a traditional treatment approach has limited utility. Documentation of health issues over time and clinical notes putting the clinical argument for release into the community have been used in many cases where clinicians are concerned about the wellbeing of a detained asylum seeker. The statement that within a damaging environment treatment is fundamentally problematic is powerful but puts clinicians in an ethical dilemma where they are potentially clinically compromised. This certainly creates stress for clinicians with the system who have raised issues of the need for external supervision and support and have noted how difficult it can be to resist taking up simplistic treatment approaches. Advocacy in this situation has been personally demanding and some have experienced vicarious traumatisation and been unable to continue. Supporting nonprofessional advocates and volunteers has also been an important role with many not experienced in dealing with high levels of distress and suicidality (Mares & Newman, 2007).

For mental health clinicians the traditional model of trauma and recovery is challenged in the detention context. The model of PTSD, while it has provided a label for making sense of individuals' experiences, has less utility when talking about trauma across a whole community or group of individuals. Trauma for asylum seekers occurs in a particular sociopolitical context and has motivated the attempt to find a safe haven and re-establish social functioning and identity. There will also be cultural variations in the expression of distress and experience of trauma and the need to explore this in a framework that is broader than that of western diagnostic approaches. This should also translate into interventions at the sociopolitical level, which transcend the individualistic psychological models of western psychology.

For research teams the issues of working with detained asylum seekers necessarily created conflict with government, who did not readily grant access to the population and attempted to question the credibility of the researchers involved and their conclusions that mandatory detention is harmful (Newman, Dudley, & Steel, 2008). Government questioned research findings about the harmful effects of detention and made accusations of intrinsic 'bias' and unethical behaviour of the research team. A body of research evidence, both national and international, were discussed. Researchers found themselves needing to raise issues of academic freedom and the right to highlight research findings. Direct involvement of government in an attempt to discredit research is a serious matter and had significant impact on the individuals involved. It also brought into focus the political complexity of undertaking research in a politicised environment and ethical issues of potential adverse impact on participant detainees. The findings of high rates of mental disorder among detainees could be used as an argument against acceptance of refugee claims in individual cases. This also contributes to possible underreporting of psychological distress adding to difficulties in interpreting results.

The criticism of academic bias ignored the convergence of findings across several studies and sought to discard robust findings that did not match a particular political position. For those in research the importance of continuing to document and publicise findings in this area remains central, particularly when results should be taken into account in discussion about policy reform and better practice. Steel and Silove (Steel,

Momartin, Bateman, Hafshejani, & Silove, 2004) argued that there is a professional imperative to investigate and report on these issues and that the research agenda should be carried on independently of government, if necessary with appropriate university ethics support. The university may offer independent review of planned research that is able to focus on the quality of the proposal and the ethical issues and do so independently of government and a political process, which may have strong opposition to possible research findings.

There are serious questions here about the values underlying all research activities and whether these should be made explicit. Research on detained populations needs to be particularly clear that it is not divorced from consideration of the appropriateness of detention and the political system in which detention occurs. In this sense research cannot be value-free and needs to describe those values and the way in which they influenced the setting of a research agenda. Researchers have a strategic role in highlighting the predicament of detained asylum seekers by both documentation of mental health impacts of detention and offering critique of detention policy and practice (Kirmayer, Rousseau, & Cepeau, 2004). Conducting research in the face of resistance and sometimes more blatant attempts at censorship of results is difficult (Schweitzer & Steel, 2008) but arguably there is a moral imperative to examine issues of human rights abuse and mistreatment of vulnerable groups. Issues of informed consent and possible negative consequences to participants are serious and remain complex in a detention context where individuals need to be fully aware of the research questions, process and consequences of participation. Mental health research often works with vulnerable groups including those detained in other contexts, where these issues are central.

It is imperative that detainees are informed about any possible negative consequences of participation in research including raising anger and punitive treatment from detention staff and officials, which may have a negative impact on their assessment process. There is also a risk that detainees conclude that cooperation and participation in research will somehow have a positive impact on their asylum claim process or improve their access to treatment and support. Researchers need to make clear statements as to the risk of participation and the lack of immediate benefit to detainees.

Current Discussion

Immigration detention has once again become a key political issue in Australia following a period of relative calm within the system. Increasing numbers of boat arrivals have prompted a political debate about factors influencing asylum seeking and those that might deter it. The argument on both sides of politics is based on an agreement that there needs to be regulation of unauthorised arrivals and that mandatory detention is necessary. In the face of increasing numbers of detainees, many with a history of torture and trauma and significant numbers of unaccompanied minors, concerns have again been raised about the mental damage caused by detention and the impact on children. Seemingly the evidence previously gathered about these issues has not been referred to as a guide to current planning. Attempts to provide psychological support and increase mental health services face the issues discussed above about the difficulties of treating in a damaging environment. Increasing numbers of 'failed' asylum seekers and long-stay cases will have a major impact on the operation of detention centres and the rates of protest, disturbance and mental disorder. Attempted suicides and suicidal behaviour are increasing and comments have again been made that 'bad behaviour' will not be tolerated and asylum seekers will face criminal charges in some situations. The challenge appears to be one of recreating some level of psychological and empathic understanding of the plight of the asylum seeker and of the impact of mandatory detention. A trauma informed model of care is essential and should underlie policy reform and service provision. Future research needs to include understanding of the process of recovery from detention, the impact of models of community-based asylum processing and issues for groups of particular vulnerability such as minors. Research ethics need to focus on the importance of translation of findings concerning risk and recovery into services and clinical programmes that contribute to the wellbeing of refugees. Documentation of harm and psychological distress has raised awareness of the harm of immigration detention but research should move towards a broader approach to models of psychosocial recovery and functioning.

References

Dudley, M. (2003). Contradictory Australian national policies on self-harm and suicide: The case of asylum seekers in mandatory detention. *Australasian Psychiatry, 11*, s102–108.

Green, J.P., & Eagar, K. (2010). The health of people in Australian immigration detention centres. *Medical Journal of Australia, 192*, 65–70.

Kirmayer, L. J., Rousseau, C., & Cepeau, F. (2004). Research ethics and the plight of refugees in detention. *Monash Bioethics Review, 23*, 85–92.

Mares, S., & Newman, L.K. (2007). *Acting from the heart: Australian advocates for asylum seekers tell their stories.* Sydney, Australia: Finch.

Newman, L.K., Dudley, M., & Steel, Z. (2008) Asylum, detention and mental health in Australia. *Refugee Survey Quarterly, 27*, 110–127.

Schweitzer, R., & Steel, Z. (2008) Researching refugees: Methodological and ethical considerations. In P. Liamputtong (Ed.), *Doing cross cultural research: Ethical and methodological perspectives, Social Indicators Research Series, Vol. 34* (pp. 87–101). Dordrecht, the Netherlands: Springer.

Silove, D., Steel, Z., Susljik, I., Frommer, N., Loneragan, C., Brooks, R., … Harris, E. (2006). Torture, mental health status and the outcomes of refugee application among recently arrived asylum seekers in Australia. *International Journal of Migration, Health and Social Care, 2*, 4–14.

Steel, Z., Momartin, S., Bateman, C., Hafshejani, A., & Silove, D. M. (2004). Psychiatric status of asylum seeker families held for a protracted period in a remote detention centre in Australia. *Australia and New Zealand Journal of Public Health, 28*, 527–537.

Sultan, A., & O'Sullivan, K. (2001). Psychological disturbances in asylum seekers held in long term detention: A participant-observer account. *The Medical Journal of Australia, 175*, 593–596.

CHAPTER

10

On Secrets and Lies: Dangerous Information, Stigma and Asylum Seeker Research

Deborah Zion

Developing countries host four-fifths of the world's refugees. Despite its wealth, high standard of living, and small numbers of people arriving without protection visas, Australia has been heavily criticised for its treatment of one of the world's most vulnerable populations — namely, those seeking refuge from war, torture and other forms of violence and discrimination. At the heart of its official policy is mandatory detention, whereby all those arriving by boat without valid documents are incarcerated, often for considerable periods of time. The detention of asylum seekers began in 1989, when a group of Cambodians arriving by boat were the first to be detained to await processing of their claims for refugee status (Lusher, Balvin, Nethery, & Tropea, 2007). In 1992, *mandatory* detention policy of those arriving without a visa by boat was introduced. The subsequent conservative government, led by John Howard, used mandatory detention in a new way, as a deterrent to those seeking refuge, rather than as a means of processing alone (Zion, Briskman, &

Loff, 2009). This regime continues at the time of writing under the Labor government led by Julia Gillard.

Despite the fact that Australia is a signatory to the Refugee Convention and that UNHCR guidelines state that detention is inherently undesirable, many asylum seekers have been detained for very considerable lengths of time. By 2001, almost 3000 people were held in detention centres like Woomera, Baxter and Curtin, awaiting determination of their visa status (Zion et al., 2009). In 2005, over 100 of those detained had been so for over three years (Mares, 2002). While detention centres such as Villawood and Maribyrnong were situated in Sydney and Melbourne respectively, the majority of prison facilities, such as Baxter, Woomera and Curtin were situated in remote and inhospitable parts of Australia. Other asylum seekers were incarcerated outside Australia as part of the so-called 'Pacific Solution' on Manus Island in Papua New Guinea or on Nauru, so that their legal claim for refugee status became harder to process.

This regime continues on Christmas Island. Despite changes to the asylum seeker system, there are still many persons incarcerated waiting for visa determination. In July 2011, there were more children in detention than there had been at any other time (Asylum Seeker Resource Centre, 2011).

Ethical issues concerning research into the effects of isolation and human rights deprivation — characteristics of the detention system — form the bedrock that underpins this article. In particular, I will discuss issues that arose out of a study investigating healthcare provision for asylum seekers. While such issues are ongoing, this discussion covers the period between 2005 and 2008 when persons were detained both onshore and offshore. More specifically, the material presented here is drawn from testimony of health care professionals about detention centres like Curtin, Baxter and Woomera. In these centres, conditions were harsh. Detainees complained about violence committed by guards, and about lack of access to the basic needs of life. Another major factor that caused distress was indeterminate length of detention. Above all, they complained about the isolation, not just from visitors but also from the oversight of due legal and administrative process.

Inaccessibility, both geographical and administrative, also made it difficult for researchers to document the conditions of detention. However, evidence emerged from government inquiries, court records and the testimony of asylum seekers who finally received visas that portrayed the detention setting as one in which human rights — including the right to health — were hard to access (Briskman, Latham, & Goddard, 2008).

Enjoyment of the right to health is particularly significant, not only because it is the foundation to a flourishing life, but also because it is intimately connected with other rights. That is 'the factors and conditions which protect and promote the right to health … shows the right to health is dependent on and contributes to, the realisation of many other human rights' (UNHCR, 2007) such as water, shelter and basic political and economic freedoms. Therefore, an investigation into health and healthcare had the potential to be highly significant in its ability to reveal the political landscape of the detention system.

The investigation of the right to health in detention is also underpinned by a more general research imperative. Correa-Velez and Gifford (2007) point out the perils inherent in not researching and recording the state of asylum seeker health and wellbeing, and how the ensuing silence further contributes to rights deprivation. They state:

> When it comes to health and human rights, more often than not asylum seekers do not count. Asylum seekers are an invisible underclass. Fleeing from their own countries they are increasingly becoming invisible noncitizens making up a portion of other nation-state populations (p. 278).

Correa-Velez and Gifford (2007) rightly suggest that the way in which obstacles have been set in the path of asylum seeker research and the lack of access to data has stifled informed discussion about the effects of detention, and the development of human social policies when people are awaiting refugee determination. In the space created by this silence, discourse has arisen based upon prejudice, fear and stigma, rather than upon evidence and rigorous discussion of political obligation, human rights, and health.

In this chapter I will describe a research project that attempts to address the silences within this discourse and examine the ethics of healthcare provision for asylum seekers in Australia. In particular, I will focus upon ethical issues that arise when researchers hear stigmatising and dangerous information. Much of this information still cannot be discussed openly. In order to protect all concerned, I have created a researcher called 'Dr Rachel Forbearance', who will share with us one of her many discoveries.

The Ethics of Healthcare Provision for Asylum Seekers in Australia: 'A Research Project'

Between 2005 and 2008, Dr Rachel Forbearance conducted a large number of interviews with nurses, doctors, psychologists and social workers, who had worked with detained asylum seekers. She entered a world in which the rule of law seemed suspended, rights were inaccessible, and violence and arbitrary punishment were the rule. For example, one nurse, 'Barry' reported that:

> I was in the pub one night and one of the guards was bragging how he'd 'took the cunt to the ground and punched his head in', and the guards would, they'd totally abuse their power. There was no real selection process for guards. And they policed the kitchen, and people were not allowed to go back for seconds, and no provision was made for particular dietary requirements and things like that. They weren't allowed to take food back into their dongers [huts]. The guards used to say horrible things, and I would hear them say 'go back to where you fucking came from if you don't like it here' and that sort of stuff. There was a lot of psychological abuse, for example if a detainee, a refugee had misbehaved or threatened

> to kill themselves, they would be incarcerated, they would have this white jacket put on them, their underwear would be removed, it was the most undignified experience, and they would be deprived of their cigarettes, visits from other refugees, and it was just appalling. Physical abuse, I mean one cheeky refugee, and cheeky in a nice way, was being a bit cheeky one day, so they took him to the ground and broke his arm.

It seemed important to make this world known to others, especially at a time when asylum seekers were vilified in the Australian media. However, 'Dr Rachel' found herself faced with an ethical quandary she had never faced before. Some of the things she heard made her worry that highly vulnerable and already stigmatised asylum seekers might be, in a real sense, betrayed by her revelations.

Several stories were troubling. In what follows I will focus on one. A series of health care providers described the misuse of the drug Panadeine Forte, which was supposed to be prescribed for pain, but was actually being given to alleviate mental suffering. This information seemed important, not least because of the addictive properties of codeine, but also because it highlighted both the terrible conditions of detention and the lack of appropriate ways to alleviate them. It also accentuated issues related to 'dual loyalty' conflict, through which health care providers were required to subordinate the interests of patients to those of the state (International Dual Loyalty Working Group, 2003). Therefore, many clinicians found themselves in situations whereby in abiding by the rules of the detention setting, it was impossible to give their patients appropriate treatment.

Nonetheless, Dr Rachel felt uneasy about making such information (and other information that she had heard) known. The government at the time was running an effective scare campaign which scapegoated asylum seekers, ascribing to them unreasonable blame for social ills and equating them with terrorists. The former prime minister, John Howard, exemplified these views when he stated that:

> I am not saying that in particular cases people on these boats are terrorists or have terrorist links ... What I am saying is that ... unless you have a proper processing system nobody has any way of determining whether they are or not. (as cited in Zion & Loff, 2008)

Asylum seekers were also characterised as 'queue jumpers, 'illegals' and cheats, shut out of the moral and social world and therefore considered unworthy of empathy and respect (Reidpath, Chan, Gifford, & Allotey, 2005).

Reidpath et al. (2005) suggest that central to this process was the construction of asylum seekers as people who were unworthy of community membership. Thus their behaviours could not interpreted through the same lenses of understanding as others who belonged, and were seen as worthy of belonging, within the social community in which they were physically situated. Reidpath et al. state:

> The government has systematically managed the social exclusion of the on-shore arrivals by marking these asylum seekers as people unworthy of community membership or the sharing of social resources. (p. 481)

The stigmatisation of asylum seekers and the systematic belittling of their plight engendered disquiet in Dr Rachel. Far from sympathising with the desperation and demoralisation of those misusing Panadeine Forte, she saw instead in her mind's eye the headline in the tabloid press: 'Illegals addicted to codeine'.

Dr Rachel was also concerned that the persons who would be negatively affected were not, in fact, those who had revealed the information to her. As such she was relying on 'nonparticipant information' or information received at second hand. Her ethical quandary brings up many issues that are common to both research with vulnerable and stigmatised populations, and to qualitative methodology. At the core of these are two issues central to all ethical codes: (a) informed consent, and (b) the duty of beneficence. Other ethical issues are also raised by Dr Rachel's dilemma, but in what follows I will focus on these two.

Informed Consent: The Problem of 'Nonparticipant' Information

While there is a large body of literature relating to informed consent between research participant and researcher, there is some measure of silence concerning the ethics of use of non-participant information. The use of nonparticipant information is not uncommon when employing in depth interviewing — the method employed here in the investigation of ethics, human rights and asylum seeker detention. However, as Pitts and Smith (2007) suggest:

> [I]nformation about ... [the nonparticipant] is being obtained without their consent and it is unclear the extent to which the decision to provide information about shared experiences is solely within the gift of one participant to impart. While it is clear that a research participant should have the right to have data pertaining to them deleted, it is less clear that a nonpartic-ipant should have the right to have information deleted about them when provided by a participant. (p. 37)

Given the ethical complexity surrounding the use of nonpartici-pant information, the decision not to interview asylum seekers themselves, but rather to rely on the evidence gained from inter-viewing those working with them requires some explanation. I will begin with a general discussion of informed consent itself, briefly examine how informed consent becomes problematic when working with vulnerable populations, and then examine how collecting information from empowered persons involved with asylum seeker detention — health care workers — both resolves and creates ethical problems.

Informed consent has been considered the cornerstone of sound ethical research practice since the evolution of the Nuremburg Code, which was developed in 1949 in response to the Nazi atrocities. The code states that 'voluntary consent of the human subject is absolutely essential' (Nuremburg Code, 1949). In subsequent documents that govern research, particularly the Declaration of Helsinki, informed consent is also fundamental in terms of protection of participants. It can be seen to act as a door which the research participant can refuse to open, or, in fact can decide to close at any time during the research process, thus affording himself or herself protection from harm, and serving as a process through which autonomy — that is, the ability to have a self-governing life — is also enhanced and protected.

Nonetheless, it is widely acknowledged that many people are not in a position to give informed consent to participate in research, and must be afforded extra protection, often by a proxy, who, after careful consideration may give consent on their behalf (Lott, 2005). Much of the literature discussing informed consent focuses on issues related to competence and lack of understanding that might make rational decision making by participants difficult, focussing on those who are mentally disabled or suffering from mental illness, and upon children as research participants.

Issues relating to choice, circumstance and enjoyment of basic economic and political liberties are, however, less well documented in discussions concerning informed consent. Nonetheless, there is some consensus that persons or populations are vulnerable in the research setting if they are denied basic political and economic rights. This vulnerability is particularly important when we consider how lack of choices might lead to exploitation in research, whereby potential participants give consent because they simply have no acceptable options other than the research process to gain access to basic rights and goods (Zion, Gillam, & Loff, 2000).

Issues related to exploitation, lack of choice and informed consent are vital to this discussion for two reasons. Firstly, they underpin the research methodology employed in this project. Secondly, they highlight why, even when obtaining information from empowered participants such as health care practitioners who worked in detention, the underlying causes of vulnerability alert us to the possibility of harm to those about whom we are seeking information.

The decision not to interview asylums seekers themselves was based upon both pragmatic and ethical concerns. For many years, researchers were barred from openly investigating the detention setting, making research within places like Baxter and Woomera only possible by stealth (Steel & Silove, 2004).

However, even if research had been permitted in the detention setting, significant ethical issues arise concerning securing informed consent from both incarcerated populations and refugees. Asylum seekers belong to both of these categories.

Informed Consent With Prisoners and Refugees

Research with incarcerated populations brings with it particular issues related to consent. I have argued elsewhere that prisoners in the criminal justice system are subject to coercive conditions, whereby they need to please guards, have limited access to health care services, and live in conditions in which violence is commonplace (Moser et al., 2004). These conditions make it difficult for the researcher to establish that a choice has been made freely, and that there are other reasonable options available outside the research setting for access to basic rights and goods (Zion, Briskman, & Loff, 2010).

Informed consent is also highly problematic in refugee research — even if the persons in question are not detained — because of the unequal power relationship between researcher and participant. Mackenzie, McDowell, and Pittaway (2007) suggest that:

> Protracted displacement situations can undermine people's sense of their own identity, their sense of self-worth, as well as their trust in themselves, thereby impairing, at least to some degree, their capacities for self-determination. (p. 303)

Further to this Hugman Pittaway, and Bartolomei (2011) suggest that:

> When entering difficult camp situations as white/western researchers, we have observed that people are so desperate for any form of assistance that they appear to agree to requests for participation in the hope that we might be able to assist them in some tangible way. This is not to suggest that people from non-Western backgrounds do not understand the principle of giving or withholding consent; rather, it reflects the quite tangible and stark power differentials between them and those who want to involve them in the research process and also the implications of the context in which consent is being sought. This makes asking for permission to interview people in such vulnerable situations or take photographs highly problematic, to say the least. (p. 8)

How do the issues raised here resonate with the ethics of research on asylum seeker detention in the Australian context? If informed consent is so easily compromised, and power imbalances so glaring, how can we fulfil the imperative to conduct such research, and return to this population 'the right to be counted' as described by Correa-Velez and Gifford (2007)?

In the project under discussion, Dr Rachel and her colleagues decided to interview empowered participants — health care providers — and to match their data with published sources and court records, to build up an accurate representation of detention, and the problems about providing health care within it. Nonetheless, as Pitts and Smith (2007) state:

> Just as data collection may involve the accumulation of information about people who have never consented to take part in research, so may the conduct of research have effects beyond those who choose to take part. (p. 38)

Pitt and Smith's (2007) insight is critical to Dr Rachel's dilemma and raises another central issue when considering ethical research practice. Namely, do we have duties of beneficence not only to participants but more generally, to those affected by our research, not to expose them to harm in the short and medium term, even if by so doing we do not report results that seem highly significant on the longer term?

The Duty of Beneficence

What then is the duty of beneficence, and what particular significance does it have when we undertake research? Many ethical and religious traditions enjoin upon us duties to help others. Singer (1996), for example, states that:

> If it is in our power to prevent something bad from happening, without thereby sacrificing anything of comparable moral importance, we ought, morally, to do it. (p. 26)

Singer is speaking in general terms. Nonetheless, the duty of beneficence, like informed consent, is considered a foundation principle when conducting research. As set out in the Declaration of Helsinki — the duty of beneficence demands that 'the interest of science and society should never take precedence over considerations related to the wellbeing of the subject' (World Medical Association, 2008). In the local context, the Australian document governing research states that researchers have a series of duties, one of which is:

> beneficence, that is, the obligations to maximise possible benefits and minimise possible harms. (The obligation to do no harm is referred to separately as non-maleficence.) Harm, in this context, extends beyond physical harm to a wide range of psychological or emotional distress, discomfort and economic or social disadvantage. Researchers exercise beneficence in assessing the risks of harm and potential benefits to participants, in being sensitive to the rights and interests of people involved in their research and in reflecting on the social and cultural implications of their work. (NHMRC, 2007)

When considering Dr Rachel's dilemma the issue of beneficence is highly significant. How then might a discussion of this concept in the research setting help resolve her problem?

When we are considering *clinical* research, the duty of beneficence creates an obligation to protect research participants, even those who have given fully informed consent, from harm, perhaps because the harms are easily identifiable and immediate. There is, therefore, considerable commentary about the need to balance individual harms against the benefits of research. Researchers, however, have an imperative to explore ways in which individuals and sub populations might not be further harmed by *any* phase of research, be it an experiment, or through publication of results.

In their discussion of stigma, Achkar and Macklin (2009) discuss the ethics of reporting research results for tuberculosis among undocumented migrants in the US. The investigators feared that such reporting might lead to discrimination against undocumented persons, and potentially to deportation when such persons were found to have tuberculosis (TB). However, given that many such persons worked in jobs involving food handling and the infectious nature of TB, not reporting such results might have serious public health implications.

The issues raised by Achkar and Macklin (2009), while based upon a clinical study, resonate with Dr Rachel's dilemma relating as they do to issues of stigma, and more significantly, to questions concerning social harm that might continue long after a research program is completed. For the TB study, however, the harm that might be caused relates to those outside of the population being studied, and the potential harm is both grave in nature, and potentially widespread. In this way, it differs from the case uncovered by Dr Rachel.

To Publish or to Report?

What then if the question of harm and benefit applies only to the population in question, as in the case of asylum seekers under discussion here? Several studies have been undertaken in Australia, which demonstrated higher rates of domestic violence in certain ethnic groups than in the general population. The anthropologist Martha Macintyre suggests that we ask the following questions before publishing detailed and community identifying results from such studies. Firstly, would publication help the victims in any way? Secondly, would publication have any influence on service provision or alter any behaviour that is causing harm? If not, Macintyre suggests that reporting to organisations or persons who might be able to assist in any way, rather than open publication, represents ethical research practice. This practice means that those most gravely affected will receive assistance, while other members of the community will not be harmed (M. Macintyre, personal communication, 2010).

Macintyre's solution resolves part of the problem under discussion here. The reporting of the findings to organisations that care for asylum seekers once they are released into the community would enable appropriate care to be given at such time. In addition, reporting to medical organisations that care for asylum seekers within the detention setting might also begin a process of discussion about appropriate use of pain relief. Nonetheless, part of the problem remains unresolved if we return to the proposition put forward by Correa-Velez and Gifford, that the experiences of asylum seekers need to enter the public discourse, and that they deserve 'the right to be counted' (Correa-Velez & Gifford, 2007).

Hugman, Bartolomei, and Pittaway (2011) provide some answer to this. In their finely nuanced discussion of ethical issues that arise in refugee research regarding sensitive information, they recount the way in which participants relate one version of events, and researchers are then told another version 'off the record'. While they cannot directly report such information, they still utilise it to inform their findings at a deeper level. They state that:

> Such information has been used carefully and confidentially within the process of analysis, to set limits on what can be

said about the particular issues, without being publically disclosed. In other words it can be used to edit material out of data, to mark it as questionable, or to make sure that other points of view on the matter are sought, but not as data itself. (pp. 665–666)

What Hugman, Bartolomei, and Pittaway are referring to here is the way in which 'dangerous information' can be used to reset research questions, as a means to scrutinise published findings, and as a way through which further research might take place in which dangerous information might be published safely. For example, researchers like Dr Rachel might be able to respond to proposed health interventions for asylum seekers upon release and suggest that issues related to drug use should receive attention without revealing stigmatising information. Researchers, cognisant of the terrible effects of detention, and the lack of appropriate resources to ameliorate suffering might also use this information to undertake research and advocacy that speaks to these points without mentioning prescription drug use per se.

Conclusion

Investigation into the lives of vulnerable populations calls for the researcher to be both methodologically creative, and ethically rigorous. In the case of Dr Rachel's dilemma, the discovery of stigmatising information concerning non-participants led to important considerations regarding informed consent and the duty of beneficence. It also leads us in other directions in terms of creating ways in which information about the misery of the detention setting, and the desperate practices within it might be reported in safety, and acted upon.

References

Achkar, J., & Macklin, R. (2009). Ethical considerations about reporting research results with potential for further stigmatization of undocumented immigrants. *Clinical Infectious Diseases, 48*(9), 1250–1253.

Asylum Seeker Resource Centre. (2001). *Get kids out of detention.* Retrieved from http://www.asrc.org.au/campaigns/1-get-kids-out-detention

Briskman, L., Latham, S., & Goddard, C. (2008). *Human rights overboard: Seeking asylum in Australia.* Melbourne, Australia: Scribe.

Correa-Velez, I., & Gifford, S. (2007). When the right to be counted doesn't count: The politics and challenges of researching the health of asylum seekers. *Critical Public Health, 17,* 273–281.

Hugman, R., Bartolomei, L., & Pittaway, E. (2011). Human agency and the meaning of informed consent: Reflections on research with refugees. *Journal of Refugee Studies, 24*(4), 655–671.

Hugman, R., Pittaway, E., & Bartolomei, L. (2011). When 'do no harm' is not enough: The ethics of research with refugees and other vulnerable groups. *British Journal of Social Work, 41*(7), 1271–1287.

International Dual Loyalty Working Group. (2003). *Dual loyalty & human rights in health professional practice: Proposed guidelines & institutional mechanisms.* Retrieved from http://physiciansforhumanrights.org/library/documents/reports/report-2002-duel-loyalty.pdf

Lott, J. (2005). Module three: Vulnerable/special participant populations. *Developing World Bioethics, 5*(1), 30–54.

Lusher, D., Balvin, N., Nethery, A., & Tropea, J. (2007). Australia's response to asylum seekers. In D. Lusher & N. Haslam (Eds.), *Yearning to breathe free: Seeking asylum in Australia* (pp. 9–29). Sydney, Australia: The Federation Press.

Mackenzie, C., McDowell, C., & Pittaway, E. (2007). Beyond 'Do no harm': The challenge of constructing ethical relationships in refugee research. *Journal of Refugee Studies, 20,* 299–319.

Mares, P. (2002). *Borderline: Australia's response to refugees and asylum seekers in the wake of the Tampa.* Sydney, Australia: UNSW Press.

Moser, D.J., Arndt, S., Kanz, J.E., Benjamin, M., Bayless, J.D., Reese, R.L., ... Flaum, M.A. (2004). Coercion and informed consent in research involving prisoners. *Comprehensive Psychiatry, 45,* 1–9.

NHMRC. (2007). *National Statement on Ethical Conduct in Human Research.* Retrieved from http://www.nhmrc.gov.au/guidelines/publications/e72

The Nuremburg Code (1949). Retrieved from http://ohsr.od.nih.gov/guidelines/nuremberg.html

United Nations High Commissioner for Human Rights. (2007). *The right to health, Factsheet 31.* Retrieved from http://www.ohchr.org/Documents/Publications/Factsheet31.pdf

Pitts, M., & Smith, A. (2007). Setting the scene. In M. Pitts & A. Smith (Eds.), *Researching the margins: Strategies for ethical and rigorous research with marginalised communities* (pp. 3–45). New York, NY: Palgrave Macmillan.

Reidpath, D., Chan, K., Gifford, S., & Allotey, P. (2005). 'He hath the French pox': Stigma, social value and social exclusion, *Sociology of Health & Illness, 27*(4), 468–489.

Singer, P. (1996). Famine, affluence and morality. In W. Aiken & H. LaFollette (Eds.), *World hunger and morality* (pp. 26–38). Upper Saddle River, NJ: Prentice Hall.

Steel, Z., & Silove, D. (2004). Science and the common good: indefinite, non-reviewable mandatory detention of asylum seekers and the research imperative. *Monash Bioethics Review, 23*(4), 93–103.

World Medical Association. (2008). *The Declaration of Helsinki- Ethical Principles for Medical Research Involving Human Subjects.* Retrieved from http://www.wma.net/en/30publications/10policies/b3/

Zion, D., Briskman, L., & Loff, B. (2009). Nursing in asylum seeker detention in Australia: Care, rights and witnessing. *Journal of Medical Ethics, 35*(9), 546–551.

Zion, D., Briskman, L., & Loff, B. (2010). Returning to history: The ethics of researching asylum seeker health in Australia. *The American Journal of Bioethics, 10*(2), 48–56.

Zion, D., Gillam, L., & Loff, B. (2000). The Declaration of Helsinki, CIOMS and the ethics of research on vulnerable populations. *Nature Medicine, 6,* 615 – 617.

Zion, D., & Loff, B. (2008). Beyond the clinical contract: Restoring asylum seeker health through advocacy and care. In A. Babacan & L. Briskman (Eds.), *Asylum seeker: International perspectives on interdiction and deterrence* (pp. 97–111). Newcastle Upon Tyne, England: Cambridge Scholars.

CHAPTER

11

Face to Face: Ethics and Responsibility

Mammad Aidani

This chapter will use Emmanuel Levinas's analysis of ethical responsibility as a point of departure for a discussion of ethics in relation to refugees. In particular it draws on my research with Iranian refugees to discuss the notion of ethical responsibility through his philosophical lens, which is fundamentally derived from Fyodor Dostoyevsky's phrase: 'we all are guilty for everything, for everybody and before everybody, and me — more than everyone else'.

For scholars working with refugees and displaced people this French phenomenologist's philosophy is important because as Jacques Derrida observes 'he never turned his eyes away from the violence' experienced by the 'foreigner, the immigrant (with or without papers), the exile, the refugee, those without a country, a state, the displaced person or population' (Derrida, 1999, p. 64). Levinas's work questions the relationship between self and other and underscores responsibility as central to ethics.

This chapter asks — What is the responsibility of the

researcher to the participant? How is responsibility towards the participant enacted? These are questions that can help to provide critical reflection about the ethics as well as the politics of the face to face relationship between the researcher and the research participants. I conclude with some critical self reflection on how Levinas's ethics of responsibility is an existential issue and one that helps us to articulate standards for our research practices by recognising that trauma and violence are not mere misfortunes of the poor but rather have a social and political dimension. Our research needs to engage with this dimension as it is often called upon by state institutions to authenticate the narratives of the refugees. In a period where doubt and cynicism surrounds refugee narratives our analytical work has enormous political value and meanings.

Research Background and Double Consciousness

Over a 10-year period I have been undertaking hermeneutic and phenomenological research on Iranian refugees in Australia, focusing in particular on their experiences of displacement, trauma, and the construction of identity in the diaspora. The research encapsulates narratives from both men and women who left Iran after the 1979 revolution as well as more recent asylum seekers.

In Australia, Iranians along with Iraqis and Afghanis have come to dominate the image of refugees entering Australia via frail rickety wooden boats. Indeed, they have been victims of voyages that have ended in horrific deaths. A boat carrying over 90 asylum seekers sank on the 15 December 2010, off the coast of Christmas Island, an Australian territory in the Indian Ocean. Most of the asylum seekers were of Iranian and Iraqi background. The vessel crashed in rough seas at Rocky Point causing the people on board to be thrown into the water. At least 30 people died and only 42 survivors were rescued.

This asylum seeker vessel gives rise to many critical reflections about the fundamental role of a refugee researcher and the ethical responsibility towards 'the other'. My cultural, linguistic and historical connection in particular to the Iranian asylum seekers on this vessel immediately roused emotions of solidarity and affinity with their plight. Indeed it was only in 1979 that as a 22 year old I too had left Iran to live a life in exile. Like many settled Iranians in Australia I could identify and understand the desperation of the asylum seekers.

Indeed, the Australian Iranian Society President, Farshad Khajhenouri, in a press release, said: 'Melbourne's Persian community felt the tragedy. Our community can associate with these people because we understand the misery they have been leaving' (*Herald Sun*, October 4, 2011). At the same time newspaper reports that 'there are dead babies, dead women and dead children in the water', (*Channel Nine News*, December 16, 2010) and the eyewitness account from Kamar Ismail, a councillor from the Shire of Christmas Island, only exacerbated the psychological abyss I felt:

> Babies, children maybe three or four years old, they were hanging on to bits of timber, they were screaming 'help, help, help', we were throwing life jackets out to them but many of them couldn't swim a few metres to reach them. (The Guardian, December 15, 2010)

This firsthand account of men, women and children drowning along the cliffs at Christmas Island did not soften antagonistic views held by a cross section of Australian society against refugees. Indeed the 'humanised images' of suffering televised over every lounge room's television screen were contrasted with images of asylum seekers being categorised as 'bogus', 'criminals', 'boat people', 'illegal', 'gate crashers', and 'back door people' who had failed to follow the appropriate legal procedures to apply for asylum in Australia (Gelber, 2003; Pickering, 2001). Thus the Iranian asylum seeker cannot go beyond these constricted images.

In this generalised construction, Iranian asylum seekers do not have a voice to speak about their subject condition and the forms of trauma they experienced. Rather, their trauma and tragic arrival on the coast is captured by a scornful and insipid metaphor, 'country shoppers', to not only imply that their claims for asylum are not authentic but also to denigrate and erase their experiences of suffering. Thus Iranian asylum seekers arriving by boat risk having their story contested and discredited. The perception of an Iranian asylum seeker as a 'country shopper' represents a paradigm that reifies the oppressive actions of the Iranian authoritarian state and ignores its atrocities. As such it fails to account for the ways in which the atrocities of the state itself create and produce preconditions for people to seek desperate means for asylum. In a sense, the arrival of Iranians 'illegally' by boats, I suggest, can be seen as a testimony of the tragedy and everyday brutality of life in Iran and the refugees are the very antithesis of the popular constructs represented of them in the media. Moreover the arrival of 'illegal' boats on Australia's shores, of mainly 'Middle Eastern' asylum seekers, needs to be considered in relation to the broader human rights abuses perpetuated in Iran, Afghanistan, and Iraq, as they do not operate in isolation from political and historical contexts. And, as such, 'illegal' asylum boats are a direct consequence of political and historical phenomena. Put in another way, Iranian 'illegal' asylum seekers do not exist in a vacuum and are not devoid of historical references but are bound to the contexts in which they are created.

As an Iranian and a scholar of refugee studies the dehumanised representation of the arrival of every 'asylum seeker boat' reported in the media has made me feel alienated and estranged, as if I've been placed 'simultaneously between two looking glasses, each presenting a sharply different image of himself' (Stonequist, 1961). Furthermore, this estrangement has promoted an experience and feelings of a dual identity in line with Du Bois' concept of a *double consciousness*: 'this sense of always looking at one-self through the eyes of others, of measuring one's soul by the tape of a world that looks on in amused contempt and pity' (Ernest, 1966).

This double consciousness I feel, in a sense, is Levinas's *stranger* — the one who is the 'exterior to me', the 'stranger [*l'Etranger*] ... who disturbs the being at home with oneself [*le chez soi*]' (Levinas, 1991, p. 39) and remains the *other* as we can never actually grasp the *being* of another person. In saying this, however, I do not wish to argue that the stranger remains totally defamiliarised and unknown to us but rather, as Levinas attests, 'comprehension of the other is therefore a hermeneutic, an exegesis' (Levinas, 1972, p. 31). In other words, an understanding of otherness, an ethics towards the other, can occur through interpreted mediations of narrative. This profound insight can be extended to shed light on how we as researchers respond to the narratives of refugees and interpret the ethical issues involved.

Ethics as an Exchange of Memories

Academics working on research with refugees are often confronted with many complexities that relate to how interview questions should be formulated and the interview itself is conducted. Indeed, many studies have revealed the ambiguities and vulnerability experienced by some researchers when conducting interviews with refugees, in particular in relation to how they address queries to their research participants. Many researchers, as well as university ethics committees, are concerned about 'triggering' the trauma experienced and find it difficult to open up conversation and discussion about the pre- and indeed post-asylum trauma.

This issue is cogently reflected in a study conducted with refugees in the UK where it was believed by the researchers that the refugees were too vulnerable to answer questions relating to their trauma. The researchers' paternalistic views were challenged by one refugee when they stated: 'You ask what you want. I will tell you what I don't want to answer. Until you ask I don't know whether I will tell you or not' (Stevenson & Willot, 2006, p. 4). In the light of this contention and with respect to my research, I too have felt the trepidation and anxiety involved in establishing rapport and trust with the participants. At no point in my research do I take my shared cultural, linguistic and historical background with the participants for granted as I am acutely aware that these 'shared' characteristics can also give rise to issues of mistrust, distress and suspicion.

This relationship of 'shared identity', I suggest, can also be characterised as an intersubjective encounter, an encounter that is framed in terms of an 'exchange of memories' (Ricoeur, 1996, p. 7). This exchange of memories, I suggest, stems from a cultural and historical bond that is constructed not on the basis of being an 'empathetic' researcher but on the basis of a shared history and a shared language with the research participants, thus making it a two-way recognition of specific histories of persecution, trauma, and displacement. It is this 'exchange of memories' that increases the ease with which participants tell their stories of loss, and human rights abuses.

Indeed, this nuance became evident during my interview with an Iranian man who described the human suffering in Evin prison:

> In Evin, you know Evin … I was given a brown blanket and had nothing else to sleep on. I was sore and hurt all over my body from the torture. They told me that all my family was dead and had been killed except for my sister. I really believed them; you know what it's like there. You know that, we can expect anything from them; they have lost their *insanieyt* (humanity). In that moment I was visited by a green angel. It came from under the brown blanket. In this horrible condition, with the vulgar language of the torturers, this beautiful green angel was smiling at me and dancing. It was this angel that helped free me.

While it is obvious that this participant has experienced a form of psychosis during his time in prison, it is not this issue, of seeing a green angel, that I want to draw attention to but rather to his regular reference of 'you know'. This 'you know' can be characterised as a form of bearing witness to his suffering but also a medium through which to situate the 'truthfulness' of the story. This 'you know' is an understanding of the intercultural dialogical relationship that shaped the way the participant narrated his story to me. While I have not been in Iran for over 30 years the participant does not feel that he has to 'contextualise' and provide 'explanations' of his narrative for he believes that all Iranians whether in exile or not have 'indelible' traces of their country's history and suffering in their memory.

It is through this intersubjective encounter that the participant has created the conditions for basic solicitude (Ricoeur, 1992, p. 191) and demands reciprocity and responsibility towards their trauma narrative without it being used for sentimental platitudes, passive consumption and appropriation. To this end, Levinas posits that we are not asked to feed the hungry and destitute with 'a gift of the heart but [rather] of bread from one's mouth, of one's own mouthful of bread' (Levinas, 1978, p. 74).

It is at this point, I contend that, refugee stories of trauma and suffering are limited if the researcher is not informed by a cultural memory of the individual's narrative; that is, one needs to know the other 'from the inside' (Derrida, 2004, p.14). As Levinas reminds us with reference to the suffering of the other, one must commit to the other by 'having the other-in-one's-skin' (Levinas, 1999, p. 161). This relationship, I suggest, can only be established in an ethically meaningful manner when we researchers 'answer' to the call of the refugee — the other; that is, without becoming a victim of our own compassion for refugees. As I have examined in my book (Aidani, 2010), we as researchers need to continually ask the existential question: what can/must I do?

Answering the Call and Ethical Responsibility

After every interview I conduct with a refugee I experience a psychological discomfort and most disturbingly a claustrophobia that makes it profoundly difficult for me to return to the trauma narratives I have recorded. Indeed at the heart of this difficulty and tension lies the question of my responsibility to the trauma narratives of the participants. In other words, do we as researchers have a responsibility towards refugees in our studies beyond the 'academic research'? To answer this question I wish to invoke the famous words of Jean-Paul Sartre who commented, 'you are perfectly free to leave that book on the table. But if you open it, you assume responsibility for it' (Sartre, 1988, p. 56). Thus the very nature of our research, I argue, compels us with a responsibility, of ethicality, as Levinas so cogently defines ethics:

> ethics is no longer a simple moralism of rules which decree what is virtuous. It is the original awakening of an I responsible for the other, the accession of my person to the uniqueness of the I called and elected to responsibility for the other. (Levinas, 1969, p. 182)

For Levinas, responsibility towards the other precedes our freedom. Freedom is not the core of subjectivity. But as Levinas writes, 'freedom can here be thought of as the possibility of doing what no one can do in my place; freedom is thus the uniqueness of that responsibility' (Levinas, 2000, p. 181). In Levinas's view before we action our freedom we have to transcend ourselves and be responsible for the other, and to respond to the face of the other. It is through this responsibility that we find the ethical self.

This responsibility for the other receives scant attention in the literature regarding the ethics of research with refugees. Rather the literature is dominated by issues relating to 'consent, confidentiality and trust, risk to researchers and potential harm to participants' (Pittaway, Bartolomei, & Hugman, 2010, p. 232). It should, therefore, not come as a surprise that I am arguing that these issues, while important, do not however go far enough to capture the complexity involved in our relationship with refugees and that they fail to locate the notion of subjectivity in terms of ethics as responsibility for the other, and a 'commandment to giving and serving' (Levinas, 1985, p. 119). By this I mean Levinas's 'substitution'; that is, putting oneself in the other's place — or as Iranians say 'putting yourself in their shoes' — without appropriating their authentic needs and aligning it with our own. In *Otherwise than Being*, Levinas says:

> Responsibility, the signification of which is non-indifference, goes one way, from me to the other. In the saying of responsibility, which is an exposure to an obligation for which no one could replace me, I am unique. Peace with the other is first of all my business. (Levinas, 1998, pp. 138–139).

It is my belief, therefore, that Levinas's *substitution* is of far greater relevance to our ethical situatedness than the concept of moral obligation advocated by some frameworks on ethics of research with refugees (Pittaway et al., 2010). Some researchers draw attention to the reality that the 'power imbalances between researchers and participants raise complex ethical issues' such as refugees constantly seeking assistance from researchers for themselves or their relatives (Pittaway et al., 2010, p. 232). For Levinas ethics itself stems from the process of the face-to-face encounter between researcher and participant and it is the power inequalities and hierarchal relationships which themselves define the self and its responsibility towards the other. For Levinas the face of the other is without power and vulnerable:

> The other concerns me in all his material misery. It is a matter, eventually, of nourishing him, of clothing him. It is exactly the biblical assertion: Feed the hungry, clothe the naked, give drink to the thirsty, give shelter to the shelterless. The material side of man, the material life of the other, concerns me and, in the other, takes on for me an elevated signification and concerns my holiness. (Robbins, 2001, p. 52)

Here, phenomenologically speaking, we can openly see that ethical responsibility starts at the level of being responsible for the material needs of the other. For Levinas, ethics is about responding to the other's material needs — feeding the hungry, clothing the naked, giving shelter to the homeless — these are the responsibility of all. And for Levinas, these are not 'ethical dilemmas'.

Our ethical situatedness in relation to the research participants compels us to answer their call to meet their basic material needs, as an ethics towards the other precedes knowledge and takes priority over politics, culture, religion and the 'ethical standards' imposed by institutions (Pittaway et al., 2010). Levinas frames the terms of this responsibility in the following way:

> I have been speaking about that which stands behind practical morality; about the extraordinary relation between a man and his neighbour, a relation that continues to exist even when it is severely damaged. Of course we have the power to relate ourselves to the other as to an object, to oppress and exploit him; nevertheless the relation to the other, as a relation of responsibility, cannot be totally suppressed, even when it takes the form of politics or warfare. Here it is impossible to free myself by saying, 'It's not my concern'. There is no choice, for it is always and inescapably my concern. (Hand, 1989, p. 247)

Ethical Reflections and Politics

It is on this point that I want to shift back to a critical self reflection of the boat tragedy that I discussed earlier in this chapter. The faces of the other are always present to me and the ethical responsibility for the other is tied to how I respond to their call. I want to point to an ethical enquiry that my family undertook in relation to the boat tragedy. This involved sending a letter to the Australian Minister for Immigration and Citizenship asking for specific information relating to the welfare of the survivors, the orphaned children, in particular relating to Iranian orphan Seena. Our question, similar in nature to the one posed by Australian Broadcasting Corporation reporter, Wendy Carlisle: Why was a traumatised boy left in an overcrowded detention centre, with substandard care, for over two months? And, indeed, against the advice of leading psychiatrists who 'lodged a complaint with the human rights commission claiming Seena's return to [Christmas] Island detention breached UN conventions' (*The Age*, February 18, 2011).

This tragedy and the lack of public accountability by the government shaped the ethical intention of this action towards the survivors. The intention of the letter was to make the government accountable and disclose what the status of the survivors was, in particular the plight of the orphaned children. The ethos of this ethical intention was to respond to the ethical complacency and alienation prevalent in our society and not to succumb to the government's representation of the other — the refugee — as an abstract category, but one whose suffering deserves recognition and responsibility. Thus this action is a mode of witnessing the aberrations of the state, an ethical questioning of state institutions and their response to human rights, and indeed a profound questioning of its solicitude towards the surviving refugees.

Thus it is difficult at this point not to return to Levinas's work for more sharp insights as to how to think critically about the political response we received from the government in relation to our enquiry. Levinas reminds us that public institutions need to be examined and made accountable in relation to their ethical relationship with the other. He observes with profound insight, as if he was commenting on the indignity of the Australian detention system for refugees:

> For me, the negative element, the element of violence in the state, in the hierarchy, appears even when the hierarchy functions perfectly, when everyone submits to universal ideas. There are cruelties which are terrible because they proceed from the necessity of the reasonable order. There are, if you like, the tears that a civil servant cannot see: the tears of the Other. (Levinas, 1996, p. 23)

Levinas reminds us that the liberal democratic state must be constantly checked and examined for its intrinsic violence. In particular in a liberal state this checking is always possible because citizens are free to ask 'whether its [the state's] own justice really is justice' (Mortley, 1991, p. 19). Furthermore, this questioning is made possible by the free press, as well as institutions and citizens who are free to criticise injustice:

> You know the prophets of the bible, they come and say to the king that his method of dispensing justice is wrong. The prophet doesn't do this in a clandestine way: he comes before the king and he tells him. In the liberal state, it's the press, the poets, the writers who fulfil this role. (Levinas, 1996, p. 23).

Thus Levinas is seeking to articulate and provide us with clues about how to inform our actions and our relationship to the other. Indeed he is telling us, the researchers, the writers, the intellectuals in a liberal society to speak out; not to keep silent; to write and to speak to power; and to check the ethics of the politics being practiced. For Levinas, speaking out and demanding an ethical relationship with the other, demanding that the government sees justice through the other's eyes is an ethical responsibility that should inform the structure of our research.

The words that I heard again and again from Iranians at the height of this tragedy were the probing of an old Persian proverb: '*Agar ensane kori ra didi ou ra lagady bezan; chera to bayad ba ou mehrabntar az khoda bashy?*' ('If you see a blind man, kick him; why should you be kinder than God'). Indeed this proverb speaks volumes about their recognition of the lack of care and good will that they will receive towards their predicament and they have no expectation of receiving hospitality. It was self evident to any reasonable person that someone who had been 'kicked around by God' was not going to receive understanding shaped by generosity and care.

Conclusion

This chapter has only scraped the surface of this complex subject and Levinas's philosophy challenges us to look differently with a new lens to issues and relationships that we so often see as 'ethical dilemmas'. It is my view that researchers need to move beyond the arguments of 'ethical dilemmas' and embrace the Levinasian notion of ethical responsibility without demeaning it by seeing it as impractical. But rather, I believe, Levinas offers us ways to respond to the notion of ethical responsibility in our face-to-face encounter with the other. From a Levinasian perspective the face-to-face encounter with our research participants demands that we see and respond to their suffering not just with compassion but also through social and political justice. This requires the ethical linking of compassion and social justice — that we recognise the political implications of their suffering, and the violence and trauma experienced.

The conventional opening phrase of Iranian stories accrues value when encountered with the words of Levinas: '*yekii boud, yekii naboud, gheyr az Khoda hich kas naboud*' ('There was being and nonbeing, there was none but God') … 'This is because I am responsible for a total responsibility, which answers for all the others and for all in the others, even for their responsibility' (Levinas, 1985, p. 95).

References

Aidani, M (2010). *Welcoming the stranger: Narratives of identity and belonging in an Iranian diaspora.* Melbourne, Australia: Australia Common Ground.

Asylum seekers die as boat sinks off Australia's Christmas Island. *The Guardian*, 15 December, 2010. Retrieved from http://www.guardian.co.uk/world/2010/dec/15/asylum-seeker-boats-capsizes-australia-christmas-island?intcmp=239

At least 28 die in Xmas Island boat crash. *Channel Nine News*, December 16, 2010. Retrieved from http://news.ninemsn.com.au/national/8183497/deaths-feared-after-asylum-seeker-crash

Christmas Island tragedy: Screams, yells and then they drowned. *Herald Sun.* October 4, 2011. Retrieved from http://www.heraldsun.com.au/news/christmas-island-tragedy-screams-yells-and-then-they-drowned/story-e6frf7jo-1225971787413

Derrida, J. (1999) *Adieu to Emmanuel Levinas* (P.A. Brault & M. Naas, Trans.). Stanford, CA: Stanford University Press.

Derrida, J. (2004). *Deconstruction in a nutshell: A conversation with Jacques Derrida.* New York, NY: Fordham University Press.

Ernest, A. Jr. (1996). On the reading of riddles: Rethinking DuBoisian double consciousness in existence. In L. R. Gordon (Ed.), *Black: An anthology of black existential philosophy.* New York, NY: Routledge.

Gelber, K. (2003). A fair queue? Australian public discourse on refugees and immigration. *Journal of Australian Studies, 1*, 23–30.

Hand, S. (1989). *The Levinas reader.* Oxford, England: Blackwell.

Levinas, E. (1969). *Totality and infinity: An essay on exteriority* (A. Lingus, Trans.). Pittsburgh, PA: Duquesne University Press.

Levinas, E. (1972). *Humanism of the other.* Chicago, IL: University of Illinois Press.

Levinas, E. (1978). *Existence and existents* (A. Lingis, Trans). The Hague, the Netherlands: Nijhoff.

Levinas, E. (1985). *Ethics and infinity: Conversations with Philippe Nemo* (R. A. Cohen, Trans.). Pittsburgh, PA: Duquesne University Press.

Levinas, E. (1996). Transcendence and height. In A.T. Peperzak, S. Critchley, & R. Bernasconi (Eds.), *Emmanuel Levinas: Basic philosophical writings.* Bloomington, IN: Indiana University Press.

Levinas, E. (1998). *Otherwise than being: Or beyond essence* (A. Lingis, Trans.). Pittsburgh, PA: Duquesne University Press.

Levinas, E. (1999). *Alterity and transcendence* (M.B. Smith, Trans). New York, NY: Columbia University Press.

Levinas, E. (2000). *God, death, and time* (B. Bergo, Trans.). Stanford, CA: Stanford University Press.

Mortley, R. (1991). *Emmanuel Levinas. In French philosophers in conversation: Levinas, Schneider, Serres, Irigaray, Le Doeuff, Derrida.* London, England: Routledge

Pickering, S. (2001). Common sense and original deviancy: News discourses and asylum seekers in Australia. *Journal of Refugee Studies, 14,* 169–186.

Pittaway, E., Bartolomei, L., & Hugman, R. (2010). 'Stop stealing our stories': The ethics of research with vulnerable groups. *Journal of Human Rights Practice, 2,* 229–251.

Ricoeur, P. (1992). *Oneself as another* (T. K. Blamey, Trans). Chicago, IL: University of Chicago Press.

Ricoeur, P. (1996). Reflections on a new ethos for Europe. In R. Kearney (Ed.), *Paul Ricoeur: The hermeneutics of action.* London, England: Sage.

Robbins, J. (2001). *Is it righteous to be? Interviews with Emmanuel Levinas.* Stanford, CA: Stanford University Press.

Sartre, J.-P. (1988). *'What is literature' and other essays.* Cambridge, MA: Harvard University Press.

Stevenson, J., & Willott, J. (2006). Cultural influences in data collection and analysis: Issues in conducting research with refugees. In J. C. P. Armstrong, R. O'Rourke & M. Zukas (Eds.), *Inter-cultural perspectives on research into adult learning: A global dialogue.* Leeds, England: Scutrea.

Stevenson, J., & Willott J. (2007). Standing on the threshold: Negotiating insider and out-sider status in cross-cultural research. In R. Mark, R. Jay, B. McCabe, & R. Moreland (Eds.), *Researching adult learning: Communities and partnerships in the local and global context* (pp. 419–426). Belfast, Northern Ireland: Scutrea.

Stonequist, E.V. (1961). *The marginal man: A study in personality and culture conflict.* New York, NY: Russell & Russell.

Island return makes Seena's trauma worse. *The Age,* February 18, 2011. Retrieved from http://www.theage.com.au/national/island-return-makes-seenas-trauma-worse-20110217-1ay7h.html

INDEX